The Citizenship Teacher's Handbook

Kate Brown and Stephen Fairbrass

continuum

Continuum International Publishing Group

The Tower Building   80 Maiden Lane, Suite 704
11 York Road   New York
London   NY 10038
SE1 7NX

www.continuumbooks.com

Main text © Kate Brown and Stephen Fairbrass 2009

Resources section

Quick glossary of terms © Tabatha Wood

Education and government © Simon Taylor

Teacher training © Simon Taylor

Unions © Simon Taylor

Curriculum © Simon Taylor

Subject associations © Simon Taylor

Exam boards © Simon Taylor

Media © Simon Taylor

Lesson planning © Simon Taylor

Inclusion – SEN and other barriers to learning © Simon Taylor

Lesson plans © Simon Taylor

Other useful websites © Simon Taylor

References © Simon Taylor

British Library Cataloguing-in-Publication Data
A catalogue record for this book is available from the British Library.

ISBN: 9781847065469 (paperback)

Library of Congress Cataloging-in-Publication Data
A catalog record for this book is available from the Library of Congress.

Typeset by Free Range Book Design & Production Limited
Printed and bound in Great Britain by Athenaeum Press Ltd., Gateshead, Tyne & Wear.

For Eileen Margaret Fairbrass JP (1936–1989) and Councillor
Charles John Fairbrass MBE, whose example provided my early
lessons in active citizenship. *SF*

For the Patels, who, in their different ways, have reminded me to be
proud of our country. *KB*

Contents

viii Contents

List of Figures

Acknowledgements

First, we would like to thank all the dedicated and creative teachers who agreed to share their work, advice and experiences with us and with you: Sir Keith Ajegbo, formerly Head Teacher, Deptford Green School; Linda Asquith, formerly Head of Citizenship and PSHE, Wakefield Cathedral High School; Aashiya Chaus, Citizenship teacher, Challenge College; Sarah Frost, Citizenship teacher, Kettlethorpe High School; Stuart George, Head of Citizenship, Didcot Girls' School; Ben Hammond, Citizenship Co-ordinator, Deptford Green School; Ben Howard, Citizenship teacher, Carshalton Boys Sports College; Brian Jacobs, Citizenship teacher, Cedar Mount High School; Alero King, Humanities, Citizenship and Sociology teacher, Queens Park Community School; Jon Mason, Head of Citizenship, Nower Hill High School; Emily Miller, Citizenship teacher, North Manchester High School for Girls; Ben Miskell, Citizenship teacher, Alder Community High School; Lucy Morgan, Teacher in Charge of Citizenship GCSE, Nower Hill High School; Nurgus Qadri, Head of Citizenship, Hanson School; James Rawling, Citizenship teacher, Kettlethorpe High School; Carrie Sharman, Head of Citizenship and Ealing Borough AST, Twyford High School; Andy Thorpe, Citizenship teacher, Bradford Academy (thanks to Bradford Academy for the use of their lesson planning pro-forma and logo); Harsharan Tung, Citizenship teacher, Belle Vue High School for Girls.

We are also indebted to Nadia Robinson from the British Red Cross, Sandy Betlem from NEAD (Norfolk Education & Action for Development), Claire O'Neill from the Education Service, Houses of Parliament, and Angie Kotler and Lee Scholtz from Schools Linking Network, who kindly agreed to explain, in their own words, how their organizations support the work of Citizenship teachers.

Finally, we would like to thank Barry Miller, Head of the School of Teaching, Health and Care at the University Centre, Bradford College, for his continued support for Citizenship Education, and the PGCE Citizenship students of the School of Teaching, Health and Care for acting as experimental guinea pigs for many of the ideas in this book.

Foreword

Why Citizenship?

In 1998, about ten years into my long headship of Deptford Green School in south-east London, I was sitting in a senior staff meeting discussing the perennial question of how to raise achievement. Deptford Green is an inner city school which, at the time, had about 50% free school meals and 60% minority ethnic pupils. It was in many ways a successful and vibrant school popular with parents. The problem that the senior members of staff were addressing was how to move academic achievement in the inner city up to the next level to compete with national averages. Another item on the agenda was a discussion about whether we should apply for specialist status, and, if so, in what area.

The items came together when an Assistant Head (now the Head of a large London school) suggested we should become a Citizenship school. Citizenship was on our minds as we had just read the report by Bernard Crick, *Education for Citizenship and the Teaching of Democracy in Schools* (QCA, 1998). The hypothesis we came up with, following this suggestion, was that inner-city pupils in relatively deprived communities can often feel disempowered. In education things are done to them and their circumstances often make them feel they have no power over their destinies. Reading the Crick report we were excited about the possibilities of student voice and active participation in the community for our students. We felt that if students were more involved in their schools and communities, with a voice to influence what happened to them, they would become more engaged in their own futures and more able to see the power and relevance of education to them.

Citizenship, of course, at that time was not on the list of subjects that schools could adopt as a specialism. As a result we embarked, led by our Assistant Head, on a journey to embrace Citizenship within our school and to persuade the Department for Schools, Children and Families that through Citizenship Education we could both empower our students as active citizens and raise their achievement. We were much supported financially in our quest by our corporate partners

UBS who were persuaded that our arguments for Citizenship chimed in with what they wanted for their employees.

Through a concentration on Citizenship Education, by appointing trained staff and creating a Citizenship department, we made real changes to our school community. We developed the student voice through a properly resourced school council and by introducing schemes such as having students as researchers in the classroom. We worked hard to empower students in the community. They campaigned successfully for better street lighting in an unsafe area, for improved leisure facilities for young people, for a safer pedestrian crossing and on a range of other issues. They went into the community, and we brought the community into school in the shape of local councillors, politicians, the police and local authority officials, to listen to their voice. We also embraced global citizenship by linking with a school in Uganda.

It is always difficult to measure the exact impact of a particular piece of work but indicators of success in the school began to take an upward turn. Exam results and behaviour improved. After our next Ofsted we were commended in the HMI's annual report. We became oversubscribed. Pupil voice became embedded in the school and significantly changed relationships.

Our campaign to become a Citizenship school eventually convinced the then Department for Education and Skills to make Citizenship a subject that could be included as part of a specialist school application. Stephen Twigg, the Minister of State for Education, said that a visit to the school had convinced him of the power of Citizenship as a driver for change.

Since then the agenda has moved on and following our work on Citizenship I was asked in 2006 by the Secretary of State for Education, to lead in the writing of a report on Diversity and Citizenship, which led to the fourth strand in Citizenship Education – Identity and Diversity: Living Together in the UK. This ties in with the new duty on schools to promote community cohesion.

I believe that Citizenship Education, well taught and resourced, can be the driver in the curriculum for both creating active citizens and citizens who have a sense of ownership and belonging in their communities. A mantra in the Children's Plan is *schools at the heart of their community*. It also talks about *the development of pupils as active and responsible citizens* and about *creating more cohesive and resilient communities*. Good Citizenship Education is key to helping us achieve these aims.

Sir Keith Ajegbo

A quick glossary of terms

AfL	Assessment for Learning
AST	Advanced Skills Teacher
Attainment Targets	These define the knowledge, skills and level of understanding that pupils of different abilities and levels of maturity are expected to have by the end of each key stage
BECTA	British Educational Communication and Technology Agency: the UK government's leading agency for Information and Communications Technology (ICT) in education
BT	Beginning Teacher: a teacher who is working in a school as part of his/her initial teacher training (ITT)
CACHE	Council for Awards in Children's Care and Education
CAL	Computer Aided Learning: applies to any learning experience that has been enhanced or supported by the use of computers
CATs	Cognitive Ability Tests: an assessment of a range of reasoning skills
CEDP	Career Entry and Development Profile: used by all new teachers to chart their progression through their teaching career
Core Subjects	English, Maths and Science: as part of the National Curriculum, all pupils must study these subjects up to Key Stage 4 (age 16)
CPD	Continuing Professional Development
CPO	Child Protection Officer
CRB disclosure	Criminal Records Bureau disclosure: it is a legal requirement that all teachers are checked against CRB records to determine their suitability to work with young people

Curriculum	The range and content of subjects taught within school
DCSF	Department for Children, Schools and Families. Formerly known as the education and children's services department of the DfES. Government department which regulates all areas of education and the National Curriculum
Diagnostic Testing	A form of assessment which highlights specific areas of strength or weakness
Differentiation	Differentiation involves teaching the same curriculum to students of all ranges and abilities using teaching strategies and resources to meet the varied needs of each individual
DT	Design Technology
E2E	Entry to Employment: schemes and training opportunities working in partnership with schools and LAs to provide suitable life skills, education and training to pupils who may have been excluded or gained very few qualifications
EAL	English as an Additional Language
EAZs	Education Action Zones: based around primary and some secondary schools. Support can include: School-Home Support Workers, extra-curricular activity centres, homework support groups in local libraries, etc.
EBD	Emotional and Behavioural Difficulties/ Disorder
EdPsyc	Educational Psychologist
EMA	Education Maintenance Allowance: a fortnightly payment of up to £60 for students who are aged 16–19 who stay on in education after they reach the end of their compulsory schooling
EMAG	The Ethnic Minority Achievement Grant: government money for supporting schools and LEAs to meet the educational needs of minority ethnic pupils
ESOL	English for Speakers of Other Languages

EWO/ESW	Educational Welfare Officer/Social Worker: a person responsible for ensuring pupils' regular attendance at school and other related issues
GCSE	General Certificate of Secondary Education: the national examination which pupils usually take in several subjects at age 16
GNVQ	General National Vocational Qualification: courses in vocational subjects such as Art and Design, Health and Social Care, etc.
G&T	Gifted and Talented
GTC	General Teaching Council
GTTR	Graduate Teacher Training Registry
HMI	Her Majesty's Inspector of schools, employed by Ofsted
HoD	Head of Department (sometimes known as Head of Subject)
HoY	Head of Year (group)
ICT	Information and Communications Technology
IEP	Individual Education Plan: a programme of support for pupils with a Statement of Special Educational Need
in loco parentis	Means 'in place of a parent'; the legal term defining teachers' responsibility for pupils in their care
INSET	In-service Education and Training for school staff
ITT	Initial Teacher Training: the period during which a teacher undertakes training to achieve qualified teacher status (QTS)
Key Stages	The National Curriculum is divided into four main stages:

	Key Stage 1	Key Stage 2	Key Stage 3	Key Stage 4
Age	5–7	7–11	11–14	14–16
Year Groups	1–2	3–6	7–9	10–11

LA/LEA	Local Authority/Local Education Authority – a division of the local government with specific responsibility for Education
LSA and LST	Learning Support Assistant and Learning Support Teacher: support staff for pupils

	with Special Educational Needs, often works with individual children in class or within designated Learning Support Units
LSU	Learning Support Unit: a department within a school set up to help students with learning and/or behavioural difficulties
MFL	Modern Foreign Languages
NLS	National Literacy Strategy
NNS	National Numeracy Strategy
NQT	Newly Qualified Teacher: a person in his or her first year of teaching who has successfully completed his/her teacher training
NRA	National Record of Achievement: a personalized folder detailing a pupil's achievement and attainment throughout his/her (secondary) school career
NT	National Tests (formerly Standard Assessment Tests SATs): tests used to show your child's progress compared with other children born in the same month. Tests taken at Key Stages 1, 2 and 3 cover the three core subjects – English, Maths and Science. GCSEs are taken at the end of Key Stage 4

Key Stage	Age National Test taken	Published
1	7	No
2	11	Yes
3	14	No
4	16	Yes

Objectives	Goals, results or improvements that the decision-maker wants to attain
Ofsted	Office for Standards in Education: the organization responsible for school inspections and assessing the quality and standards of education
PANDA	Performance and Assessment: a report generated by Ofsted to allow schools to assess their performance and make comparisons with other schools nationally
PAT	Pupil Achievement Tracker: a piece of diagnostic and analytical software produced by the DCSF/DfES to enable students'

	performance and attainment to be tracked
Pedagogy	Refers to the art or science of teaching, but also describes the strategies, techniques and approaches that teachers can use to facilitate learning
Performance Tables	The collected statistics for schools and LEAs such as results of national examinations and absence data, etc. published by the DCSF
PPA	Planning, Preparation and Assessment: at least 10% of every teacher's timetable should be free for PPA time
Programmes of Study	The content of teaching programmes laid down in the National Curriculum for each subject
PSE or PHSE	Personal and Social Education, or Personal, Social and Health Education
PSP	Personal Support Plan: personalized targets to support pupils often on the verge of exclusion
PTA	Parent–Teacher Association
QCA	Qualifications and Curriculum Authority, the body which develops the curriculum and its assessment
QTS	Qualified Teacher Status: qualification gained after successfully completing a period of teacher training needed to work in any state-maintained school
SEN	Special Educational Needs: a term used to describe a range of conditions within three main categories: Learning Difficulties, Behaviour Difficulties or Physical and Medical Difficulties
SENCO	Special Educational Needs Coordinator: the teacher with responsibility for SEN pupils within a school
SLT	Senior Leadership Team
SMART Targets	Specific, Measurable, Achievable, Realistic and Time-related: helping to monitor how targets and goals are viewed and completed
SMT	Senior Management Team: the leading members of a school or education provider
TDA	Teacher Development Agency aka Training and Development Agency for Schools:

	(formerly the TTA or Teacher Training Agency)
TLR	Teaching and Learning Responsibilities: responsibilities which impact positively on educational progress beyond the teacher's assigned role
VAK	Visual, Aural and Kinaesthetic learning styles model: refers to the preferred learning style of an individual and focuses on 'active' teaching and learning strategies

Introducing Citizenship Education

Why teach Citizenship?

If you were to ask most teachers, at the very beginning of their careers, why they wanted to teach, they would say something like 'to make a difference', 'to make a contribution', 'to help young people make sense of the world around them'. A few older teachers (but by no means all of them, one of the authors of this book is knocking on a bit) become jaded after a long career. Battered by a seemingly endless stream of new legislation around education, by myriad changes to the National Curriculum, by edicts to address multiple initiatives, they lose sight of what made them become teachers in the first place. It is no surprise that some of these teachers were, and perhaps remain, sceptical about the introduction of National Curriculum Citizenship. But teaching Citizenship is not just another initiative, adding one more meaningless 'subject' to an already overcrowded curriculum. The introduction of Citizenship Education to the curriculum marked a real change in thinking about the purpose and future of education generally. Citizenship teachers really can, and do, make a difference.

> We aim at no less than a change in the political culture of this country both nationally and locally: for people to think of themselves as active citizens, willing, able and equipped to have an influence in public life and with the critical capacities to weigh evidence before speaking and acting, to extend radically to young people the best in existing traditions of community involvement and service, and to make them individually confident in finding new forms of involvement and action among themselves. There are worrying levels of apathy, ignorance and cynicism about public life . . . we should not, must not, dare not be complacent about the health and future of British democracy. Unless we become a nation of engaged citizens, our democracy is not secure.
>
> The Crick report (1998)

The quotation above is from the introduction to the final report of the Advisory Group on Citizenship, published in 1998 and generally referred to as the Crick report, after the name of the Chairman of the Group, Professor Sir Bernard Crick. This report directly led to the introduction of the National Curriculum orders for Citizenship Education in secondary schools, in force from September 2002.

The concerns about the safety and future of democracy and civil society highlighted in the Crick report (and which Citizenship Education seeks to address) are not new. Edmund Burke (1729–1797) is credited with the phrase '*for evil to flourish it is sufficient that good men do nothing*' and Thomas Jefferson, third President of the United States (from 1801 to 1809), is said to have coined the aphorism '*the price of liberty is eternal vigilance*'. If we should doubt the veracity of these warnings, we have only to look at the rise of Nazism in 1930s' Germany for their proof. The famous words generally attributed to Pastor Martin Niemöller (1892–1984) confirm the theme:

> They came first for the Communists, and I didn't speak up because I wasn't a Communist. Then they came for the sick, the so-called incurables, and I didn't speak up because I wasn't mentally ill. Then they came for the Jews, and I didn't speak up because I wasn't a Jew. Then they came for the trade unionists, and I didn't speak up because I wasn't a trade unionist. Then they came for the Catholics, and I didn't speak up because I was a Protestant. Then they came for me, and by that time there was no one left to speak up.
>
> Pastor Niemöller

It is perhaps pertinent that many different translations and variations of Niemöller's words have been produced. The line about the incurables and mental illness is only rarely cited, and in 1950s' United States (during the McCarthyist 'witch hunts' of 'left-wing' sympathizers) the line about the Communists was routinely omitted from published versions. Even in Niemöller's original there is no mention of them coming for the homosexuals, though history tells us that the Nazis did just that.

As we were writing this book (spring and early summer 2008), Robert Mugabe was attempting to pervert the democratic process in Zimbabwe; 'stealing the election' as the media, Gordon Brown, the British Prime Minister, and others commented. It would be easy for us to be complacent and take the view that such a thing could not happen in a mature democracy like the UK. Then again, did George W. Bush really beat Al Gore in Florida in 2000 to win the US presidential election?

So what is Citizenship about?

Although concern about the future of democratic society is not new, the commitment to equip young citizens, through their schooling, through courses in Citizenship Education, with the knowledge and skills to enable them to 'be vigilant' and 'do something' and to 'speak up', is. The purpose of Citizenship Education is ultimately to contribute to the continuance and development of just and democratic societies, with vibrant and active engagement of citizens as individuals and through the various forms of civil society organizations. Citizenship Education is education about democracy, but more importantly it is education for democracy.

If democratic society is to function effectively, then people need to understand, and be able to participate effectively in, decision-making processes. They need to understand both how and why decisions are made. Every day millions of decisions are made in the world. Decisions are made, inter alia, by:

- you, and by us, as individuals
- groups of people coming together in community, social or charity organizations, from local playgroups for children to international development organizations such as Oxfam
- businesses, from corner shops to transnational corporations
- law enforcement agencies, and by courts and the justice system institutions
- local and national governments, and quasi-governmental institutions
- international bodies such as the European Union, the United Nations and the World Trade Organization

Every decision made by an individual, group or institution has ramifications for other individuals, groups or institutions. Decisions made here in the UK can have impacts upon people living many thousands of miles away; decisions made many thousands of miles away can have impacts upon us. Decisions made by a few may have consequences for the many, decisions made now may have effects far into the future. All decisions, presumably, bring benefits for some; for at least the decision maker, otherwise why would they make the decision? But decisions also have consequences or costs; and the costs are not always borne by the people receiving the benefits. In a democracy it is important that those negatively affected by decisions have a say in the decision-making process, at least equal to those who benefit.

Citizenship seeks to help young people understand the decisions of others, and how, legitimately, to challenge decisions with which they disagree. It further seeks to encourage those young people to critically consider their own decisions, and the ramifications of those decisions for others; for example, how their decisions as consumers may affect other people's livelihoods and environments.

Sometimes decisions made by others are difficult for us to understand. We may regard a particular decision as irrational, stupid and unintelligible. For the decision maker, however, that decision may be logical, natural and inevitable. If we are to understand others' decisions we need to develop skills of empathy, the ability to see the world from another's point of view. Sometimes that may be uncomfortable for us. Our politicians and our media are quick to condemn opponents, and views or actions with which they disagree, as the ravings and actions of madmen. But those views and actions, even if you and we find them morally, politically or otherwise repugnant, must have rationality for those who enact them. How much more effectively can we challenge (for example) the views of the British National Party if we actually understand their arguments? How better can we confront the actions of the 9/11 terrorists, if we can envision their thought processes, and the social and political circumstances, that led them to those terrible deeds? As the poet Robert Burns (1759–1796) wrote: *'Oh would some power the giftie gie us, to see ourselves as others see us.'*

Citizenship Education seeks to enable young people to ask questions about a whole range of issues facing the world they live in, issues that will affect their own and others' lives, and to discuss with others opinions and facts about these issues in the search for possible answers. In doing so, we hope that young people will grow into adults who, alongside their peers with different backgrounds and opinions, will continue to actively participate in the continuing development of the communities and societies in which they live.

Inevitably, Citizenship Education ventures into highly controversial and difficult subject matter. Approximately 40 years ago, Neil Postman and Charles Weingartner wrote a book called *Teaching as a Subversive Activity* (now, sadly, 'out of print', but there is a thriving market in 'second-hand' copies, from all the usual internet sources, and we recommend it to every Citizenship teacher). The passage inset overleaf is a quotation from the introduction to that book. Read it through, and in your mind substitute 'Iraq' for *'Vietnam'*, 'Al Qaeda' for *'communist conspiracy'* and so on, and then consider how prescient the original authors were. While Postman and Weingartner refer explicitly to the United States in their text, we hope you will agree that the problems that face us here in the UK are not dissimilar.

One can begin almost anywhere in compiling a list of problems that, taken together and left unresolved, mean disaster for us and our children. For example, the number one health problem in the United States is mental illness: there are more Americans suffering from mental illness than all other forms of illness combined. Of almost equal magnitude is the crime problem. It is advancing rapidly on many fronts, from delinquency among affluent adolescents to frauds perpetrated by some of our richest corporations. Another is the suicide problem. Are you aware that suicide is the second most common cause of death among adolescents? Or how about the problem of 'damaged' children? The most common cause of infant mortality in the United States is parental beating. Still another problem concerns misinformation – commonly referred to as 'the credibility gap' or 'news management'. The misinformation problem takes a variety of forms, such as lies, clichés and rumours, and implicates almost everybody, including the President of the United States.

Many of these problems are related to, or at least seriously affected by, the communications revolution, which, having taken us unawares, has ignited the civil rights problem, unleashed the electronic-bugging problem and made visible the sex problem, to say nothing of the drug problem. Then we have the problems stemming from the population explosion, which include the birth-control problem, the abortion problem, the housing problem, the parking problem and the food and water-supply problem.

You may have noticed that all these problems are related to 'progress', a somewhat paradoxical manifestation that has also resulted in the air-pollution problem, the water-pollution problem, the garbage-disposal problem, the radio-activity problem, the megalopolis problem, the supersonic-jet-noise problem, the traffic problem, the who-am-I problem and the what-does-it-all mean problem.

Stay one more paragraph, for we must not omit alluding to the international scene: the Bomb problem, the Vietnam problem, the Red China problem, the Cuban problem, the Middle East problem, the foreign-aid problem, the national defence problem and a mountain of others mostly thought of as stemming from the communist-conspiracy problem.

Now, there is one problem under which all the foregoing may be subsumed. It is the 'What, if anything, can we do about these problems?' problem.

Postman and Weingartner (1969)

We can't imagine that anyone could fail to see the continued relevance of Postman and Weingartner's text, but if you still need convincing, how about this list, drawn up in 2002 by the then Vice President for Europe of the World Bank, J. F. Rischard, of the twenty crucial problems facing the world at the beginning of the twenty-first century.

> Global warming, biodiversity and ecosystem losses, fishery depletion, deforestation, water deficits, maritime safety and pollution, poverty, peacekeeping and conflict prevention, education for all, infectious diseases, digital divide, natural disaster prevention, taxation, biotechnology rules, global financial architecture, illegal drugs, trade rules, intellectual property rights, e-commerce rules, international labour rules.
>
> Rischard (2002)

Citizenship Education starts from the belief that human beings, citizens, can do something about the multiple problems facing the world. Individuals can, and do, have a profound effect upon the world they live in. One of the biggest initial challenges for Citizenship teachers is to convince young people of this: that their opinions matter, and that they do have power to bring about change for the better. Faced with the scale of some of the world's problems young people can often feel insignificant and powerless. Citizenship Education seeks to challenge the sense of powerlessness, the sense that there is some kind of inevitability to local, national and global development. Change is inevitable; it is not the nature of the world, or of human beings, to 'stand still', but the direction of change can be profoundly influenced by our actions (or by our inaction, as Niemöller reminded us).

> A Buddhist monk once told a story on the 'Thought for the Day' slot on BBC radio. Two men were walking along a tropical beach. The tide that morning, as on every morning, had washed ashore millions of starfish. Stranded on the beach, the starfish would shrivel and die. One man bent down and picked up a live starfish, and threw it back into the sea. A few steps further and he picked up another, and threw it also into the sea. His friend was astonished. *'What are you doing? Your tiny efforts can't make a difference to all these creatures.'* The first man shrugged his shoulders and kept on walking. A few steps later he bent down, picked up a starfish, and threw it into the sea; *'Made a difference to that one,'* he whispered to himself.

Citizenship Education aims to show young people that they have the power to make a difference. Margaret Mead, a famous anthropologist, once said: *'Never doubt that a small group of thoughtful and committed citizens can change the world. Indeed it is the only thing that ever has.'* Bryan Murphy (1999) argues that *'the future for human society could be a brutal, miserable existence, as many currently predict, but it could just as well be a creative, open and humane existence. The future is not determined; it is influenced by what we do now in our various communities, in our various countries, and in common cause internationally – by the possibilities we envision and the actions we take to make our visions reality.'*

Citizenship Education – itself a controversial issue?

We have already made the point that Citizenship Education explores controversial and very difficult issues, but in fact, Citizenship Education is itself a controversial issue, and that includes defining what precisely it is. At the heart of Citizenship Education there is a tension, perhaps even a conflict, essentially between two opposing positions. The positions are not necessarily mutually exclusive, nor irreconcilable; indeed the tension may be creative and constructive. However, the tension is certainly something that we believe Citizenship teachers need to consider.

On the one hand, and as we have hopefully indicated already, is a view of Citizenship Education that sees its purpose as essentially empowering. Citizenship Education enables young people to critically analyse their society and identify its shortcomings; understand, and be able to utilize, the mechanisms through which social and political change might be achieved. A 'good citizen' in this model is an intellectually angry citizen, one who is concerned about injustice, intolerance and inequality, and is willing to act to challenge authority where necessary.

Critics of this approach to Citizenship Education, however, would see this vision as dangerously revolutionary. Instead they prefer a view of Citizenship Education that develops a very different kind of 'good citizen'. In this sense a 'good citizen' is law-abiding, respectful of peers and superiors, respectful of authority. A 'good citizen' picks up litter, helps old ladies across the road and remembers to send flowers on Mothering Sunday. A 'good citizen' raises money for charity, and does voluntary work in the community. This view of Citizenship Education sees its purpose as socialization; inculcation into the norms and values of 'decent' society, with knowledge of the key institutions of political and justice systems thrown in for good measure. Another more critical take on this approach to Citizenship Education would see it as a form of social control.

The tension over the nature of Citizenship Education was clearly demonstrated shortly after the National Curriculum for Citizenship was introduced in schools, as the UK government made preparations to engage in a war in Iraq. Hundreds of thousands (perhaps millions) of people took to the streets in 'anti-war' demonstrations across the country; among them many teenagers who 'truanted' from school to participate in the protests. A debate ensued in the press; some (including the then Secretary of State for Education, David Blunkett, a keen advocate of Citizenship Education, and the Prime Minister, Tony Blair) castigated these young people for their failure to obey the law and attend school. Others, including a number of Headteachers (who were being urged by the authorities to clamp down on, and punish, the truants), praised the young people for their willingness to stand up for what they believed was right, and challenge a government they believed was wrong. We leave it to you to consider whether a 'good citizen' is one who obeyed the rules and went to school, or one who took part in the demonstrations.

We have deliberately painted the two perspectives on Citizenship Education as extreme ends of a spectrum, to make clear the nature of the debate. In practice there is, perhaps, a more comfortable middle ground. An empowering Citizenship Education gives young people ownership of their communities/societies. With ownership may come pride in ownership, and with that pride a desire to make society decent; and maybe a self-interest in 'picking up litter'. The National Curriculum for Citizenship can be seen as encompassing elements of both perspectives on the nature of Citizenship Education, perhaps unsurprising given its origins in a committee made up of people from a range of political and social viewpoints.

For what it is worth, and as perhaps is already evident by now, we lean towards the first of the two basic models identified above. And yes, we marched to demonstrate against the war! However, lest you suspect us of too much partisanship in an unresolved debate, let us refer to Ofsted (the Office for Standards in Education, Children's Services and Skills):

> There is plenty to argue about in citizenship. Why was it introduced really? Is it about good behaviour or asking awkward questions? . . . The aims of the first National Curriculum in citizenship, and their potential for success have been the subject of much debate, and will remain contended areas. A theme pursued by critics is that the citizenship curriculum is about compliance, good behaviour and the acceptance of values rather than 'critical democracy' in which they can become engaged as active citizens. In its focus on the intentions of the National Curriculum, Ofsted disagrees with this view and sees much that takes forward the notion of 'critical democracy'. For example, Ofsted's reports have noted good practice in campaigning and challenging – including defending the status quo. When taught correctly, the National Curriculum and post-16 citizenship education encourage these elements.
>
> Ofsted (2006)

This tension over the nature of a 'good citizen' is just one of many debates surrounding Citizenship Education. Another might be whether Citizenship is, in fact, a 'subject' at all. Is it a non-subject and a waste of time and money, a distraction from the important business of teaching numeracy and literacy? Or is it more than a subject, central to our understanding of what it means to be human and live in society with other humans?

Either way, Citizenship is new and evolving. You can read more about the National Curriculum requirements for Citizenship in Chapter 2, but you should bear in mind that the subject's definition is not (and we would argue never will be) a closed issue. In this context, professional Citizenship teachers have a key role to play in defining the future of their subject. We believe that all Citizenship teachers should become reflective and critical thinkers about their subject, constantly evaluating what they are trying to do and why.

> I view Citizenship Education as nothing less than a crusade to actively engage the population in civic society. This grand aspiration is not an easy task; it is a process which involves finding solutions to empower young people, building a sense of political agency and opening minds about the world in which we share and the communities from which we stem. As Citizenship teachers, we strive to dispel apathy and provide a powerful antidote to disengagement. Many within our

(continued)

number talk about a mythical 'good citizen'; although what unites us is the noble desire to create a better tomorrow.

Student textbooks spend page after page focusing on what makes a 'good' citizen. 'Good' we are told, at least in this context, means someone who helps a friend, raises money for charity and certainly someone who sticks to the rules. But this simplistic, and somewhat reductive, view of Citizenship is actually part of the problem. Students cannot simply be 'taught' about becoming a model citizen. Moreover, the very model of a 'good' citizen should always be open to lively debate and challenge in a healthy dynamic society. A 'good' citizen is not simply a passive consumer, or for that matter an individual who blithely follows the rules without understanding. He or she is someone who is able and willing to work with others in order to campaign for their rights and the rights of others, and in doing so critically challenge (or informedly support) the status quo. Most importantly, such an individual has an insatiable desire to shape society for the better and has a drive and a body of knowledge and experience to make it happen.

A better tomorrow can never be taught as a 'how to' course in 'good citizenship'. Teachers, just like policy makers, do not have all the answers and therefore a top-down didactic style would not be fit for purpose. Lessons that resonate with young people are relevant to their life experiences. Good lessons seek to address social problems that affect young people in society, and in doing so take learning beyond the classroom and into real lives. Such active learning experiences allow students to learn about systems and processes long considered 'dry', such as the electoral process or legal systems, with an added vigour.

Older generations often seem to view negatively those that succeed them. They promote the myth of a British way of life suddenly plunged into an unnatural state of disorder by hordes of rampaging youth. It is becoming increasingly trendy nowadays to talk about our 'broken society'. Critics often hark back to a 'golden age' in which they claim young people behaved, conformed and in fact acquiesced in civic society. Yet the reality is far from as convenient and this rose-tinted view does not stand the test of scrutiny. Hitherto was an age when the notion of student voice was not characterized by vibrant student councils, but was instead seen as a distraction in the classroom that needed quashing, in favour of control. It is therefore today, rather than yesteryear, that is the educational golden age. Every day I see young people who are far from apolitical. They care passionately about issues that matter to them and their world. They have views and opinions and are crying out to express them. As a Citizenship teacher, it is my job to channel that energy, so that we can truly foster 'good' citizens who are not simply passive consumers, but active and engaged members of our diverse communities.

Ben Miskell, Citizenship teacher, Alder Community High School, Tameside

The history of Citizenship Education

There are a lot of myths about the origins of Citizenship Education, and in particular the National Curriculum for Citizenship. The most common myth is that Citizenship Education was a pet project of 'New Labour' in 1997, and specifically the brainchild of David Blunkett when he was Education Secretary. This leads also to the mythical belief that, if and when the Labour Party is removed from government by the electorate, Citizenship Education will 'disappear'.

A simple telling of the history of Citizenship Education should help to dispel those myths, but the story has already been told very well elsewhere. We can do no better than direct you to Potter (2002) for an overview of the immediate circumstances leading to the 2002 introduction of Citizenship as a National Curriculum subject. For our purposes, here are the highlights of Potter's story:

- Douglas Hurd, Conservative Home Secretary from 1985 to 1989, spoke publicly of the need for 'active' rather than 'good' citizens;
- Bernard Weatherill, Speaker of the House of Commons, was invited to chair the *Speaker's Commission on Citizenship*, and reported in 1990 (under a Conservative government) with a recommendation that Citizenship Education should be taught in schools as a 'cross-curricular theme'. There was cross-party support for this recommendation;
- Bernard Crick was invited to chair an Advisory Group for Citizenship, to review the existing provision of Citizenship Education, to evaluate its success and make recommendations for its improvement – leading to the publication of the Crick report (1998) and the establishment of Citizenship as a National Curriculum 'foundation subject' from September 2002.

However, Citizenship Education has a much longer history in the UK. Ofsted cite, as a source of information for their report *Towards Consensus* (2006), an 1885 book entitled *The Citizenship Reader.* They also say: *'At face value the National Curriculum follows a similar line to the citizenship education taught in many schools a century before. Common subject matter includes learning about the institutions of central and local government and how they work, elections and voting; and law and justice . . . What makes the current national curriculum very different from what was taught a century before is the inter-relationship of the knowledge and understanding with the other two "strands" of citizenship: enquiry and communication, and participation and responsible action. It is these active elements that make citizenship new and challenging, and so moves the curriculum away from "compliance" towards "critical democracy" in a school context'* (2006).

So, continuity and change. There has long been recognized a need for young people to understand how they are governed, how the system works. What is new, for the twenty-first century, is a recognition that young people need to be able to develop not just the knowledge of how they are governed, but the skills to participate in governance. It is impossible to divorce this changing view of the focus of Citizenship Education from wider social and political debates about the nature of democracy and governance, and the increasing complexity of our globalized governance systems.

The development of Citizenship Education is not only, or even principally, a UK phenomenon. *'The English education system was not alone in seeking an answer to big questions of the day. Concern was being expressed throughout Europe that schools give insufficient emphasis to the principles of "Education for Democratic Citizenship" (EDC). This is about "citizenship based on the principles and values of human rights, respect of human dignity, pluralism, cultural diversity and the primacy of law". Many European countries and states, individually and collectively, were working on frameworks to underpin the development of EDC, and advice and resources to support development and implementation'* (Ofsted, 2006). 'European Year of Citizenship Education' was celebrated in 2005, and we are aware of the growth of interest in, and the development of programmes of, Citizenship Education in the USA, Australia, New Zealand, Pakistan and Japan, amongst others. Citizenship Education is a growing, and global, phenomenon.

Summary

In *Teaching as a Subversive Activity* (1969) Postman and Weingartner outline their vision for a 'new education', an education in which *'the schools must serve as the principal medium for developing in youth the attitudes and skills of social, political and cultural criticism.'* In rather more basic terms, they argue that schools should enable each young person to develop their own *'built-in, shockproof crap detector'*, a tool for examining, analysing and critically evaluating the social, economic and political structures of the day.

We would argue that Citizenship Education is the logical extension of Postman and Weingartner's vision, and that the role of the Citizenship teacher is to help young people develop the skills to detect crap. But we go beyond Postman and Weingartner in saying that Citizenship teachers should help young people to develop the confidence to be able to stand up publicly and say, in loud and clear voices, 'this is crap', and further to be able to make the case for, and have the skills to implement, the process of sweeping it away and replacing it with something better. We hope you share that aim, and that this book will help you to achieve it.

Those of us engaged in the training of new Citizenship teachers are justifiably proud of the dedication and achievements of our protégées. If you are just beginning your career as a Citizenship teacher, as a PGCE trainee or NQT, you are one of a very select group. Admission to the Citizenship PGCE programmes is very competitive, and only those who demonstrate the highest potential succeed. This book is intended to help you turn that potential into accomplishment.

However, while we will be aiming to give you a whole range of information, and some practical tips, for your career as a Citizenship teacher, we do not see this book as simply being a guide on 'how to do it'. Rather, we hope to encourage you to think reflectively and critically about Citizenship Education, your own teaching and about education and schooling more generally. We know lots of Citizenship teachers who are already doing this, and some of them have kindly agreed to share some of their thoughts in this book. Their testimonies are indications of their own development as reflective practitioners in Citizenship Education, which we hope will help to inspire you.

We have indicated already that Citizenship Education is controversial in a multi-dimensional way. This book will itself have controversial content. We don't ask you to accept all of what we say as 'truth', all we ask is that you engage with the debates. We look forward to reading your books in due course, telling us which bits we got wrong!

Teaching and learning Citizenship in schools Part 1: Education for democracy and the National Curriculum

2

Democracy and the school

There is something of a paradox right at the beginning of Citizenship Education, or education for democracy. A paradox of endeavouring to teach the skills of democracy in one of most profoundly undemocratic institutions known to humankind, one of the last bastions of true dictatorship on this earth – the school. There is a cartoon passed around between Citizenship trainees and teachers picturing a balding, bespectacled teacher standing in front of an old-fashioned blackboard with line after line of text chalked up. Students sit at individual desks facing the front. The caption reads *'I expect you all to be independent, innovative, critical thinkers who will do exactly as I say.'* As teachers, we've worked with Headteachers who adopt pretty much the same attitude towards their staff.

Writing in *The Times Educational Supplement*, Fiona Clarke asks *'I wonder how pupils are expected to grasp the ideas of democracy and citizenship when they have been trapped in a totalitarian educational system which does not recognize their right to choose what they learn or how they learn it'* (2002). Her sentiment is echoed by Gearon's question, *'Can an essentially undemocratic institution, with little potential for genuine power sharing, offer a context for young people to experience democracy in action?'* (2003). There is a long tradition of academic and political thought that questions the possibility of democracy in schools, and the link between democratic education and the existence of true democracy in broader society. If you have time, we would recommend to you the work of Paulo Freire (1970) and Antonio Gramsci (in Hoare and Nowell-Smith, 1971).

Certainly, there is an inherent tension here, one that is obvious to all teachers and trainees. On the one hand we are facilitators, supporting young people to strengthen their agency and have their voice heard. On the other hand we are part of strictly hierarchical and authoritarian structures, enforcing rules in which the school's, and consequently our own, authority is expressed. The situation can be exacerbated when colleagues are unaware or even downright hostile towards 'newfangled Citizenship ideas'. Even in cases where Citizenship really is an integrated and supported part of school life, the tension still remains, and it is unlikely to go away in the near future. Multiple stakeholders, the legal responsibilities of schools and general inertia mean that the way in which schools are structured and run is not going to change overnight.

However, as part of a wide-ranging agenda of strengthening participation and democracy in society, one of the purposes of Citizenship Education is to begin the process of democratizing education and schooling (a purpose that is supported by the 'Every Child Matters' agenda, see Chapter 6). Some schools have already taken steps along a road that makes them more responsive to the wishes of, and accountable for their actions to, their students. We welcome this process. We have worked in schools where a 'them' and 'us' attitude prevails among students and staff, and it is not conducive to the personal growth, development and wellbeing of either side, nor to effective education. Schools are strengthened by shared ownership of both the strategic and daily decisions that need to be taken, and which affect the day-to-day lives of all the stakeholders in the school.

Proponents of the democratization of schools have been around for a long time. In 1969, two Danish schoolteachers, Søren Hansen and Jesper Jensen, published a highly controversial text, *The Little Red School Book*, which was subsequently translated into many languages (the English version first appeared in 1971) and sold in undisclosed numbers around the world. The reason that we do not know how many copies were published and sold is that governments were so horrified by the contents of the book that they tried to suppress it, and many copies changed hands illegally. One of the authors of this book obtained his copy from a classmate when he was 16 years old and in the sixth form. Once again we fear that if you want to read this book you will have to track down a second-hand copy.

The Little Red School Book (we've wondered whether the pun is deliberate, but probably not since it only works in English) was consciously modelled on Mao Zedong's famous little red book *Selected Quotations from Chairman Mao Zedong* (1966). Mao's original was certainly not 'little read'. An estimated 900 million copies were sold, making it the second best-selling book of all time, after the Bible, and narrowly beating the Qu'ran into third place (Ash, 2007). There's no particular reason why you need to know that, but it might be useful in a trivia quiz one day.

In France and Italy *The Little Red School Book* was simply banned. In England it was prosecuted under the Obscene Publications Act; one chapter of the book gave young people advice on sexual matters using rather graphic language, which was just sufficient excuse for the authorities to invoke legal proceedings. (Do you see what we meant in Chapter 1 about the need for eternal vigilance? Freedom of speech and publication, even in advanced democracies, cannot be taken for granted.) Only after the offending passages were excised was publication, reluctantly, allowed.

The Little Red School Book was essentially aimed at informing young people about their rights within the education system and beyond, and more importantly contained advice about how to campaign for those rights, and how to question and challenge authority. Political and religious authorities of the time regarded the book as dangerously subversive. While there is material in *The Little Red School Book* that might be considered somewhat controversial even today, it is our opinion that much of the content of the book could be seen as a blueprint for the democratization of schools, 'education for democracy', and a guide for young people towards 'active citizenship'. As the book says: *'If you want to have some say in the way things are done, to get things changed and to improve your own life at school, there are several things you should know. Democracy is built on action. This doesn't mean unconsidered actions, but active contributions to getting things changed'* (Hansen and Jensen, 1971).

We believe that this call to action applies as much to teachers as it does to students. Professional Citizenship teachers have a key role to play as 'missionaries for democracy' in schools. From your first appointment as a Citizenship NQT we encourage you to campaign and agitate, at departmental, faculty and staff meetings, and by directly approaching the Headteacher for change in this direction. If there is not a school council, make the case for one and offer to help set it up. If there is a school council, get involved with it and seek to broaden and deepen its role and influence. Constantly seek opportunities to strengthen 'student voice'. Use the requirement to teach Citizenship and democracy, and the requirements of Every Child Matters (see Chapter 6), to support your arguments. Be part of the *'open conspiracy for social change'* (Murphy, 1999).

National Curriculum Citizenship

If this book is your first introduction to Citizenship Education, by now we hope you are starting to think, '*This sounds great, but how do I actually do it, and as a Citizenship teacher, what does the law of the land require that I do?*' We aim to help you to begin to formulate your own answers to these questions in this chapter.

In England, Citizenship Education is a statutory requirement at Key Stages 3 and 4. Scotland has its own requirements for Citizenship Education as part of its *Curriculum for Excellence*, and in Wales many Citizenship themes are addressed through the *National Curriculum for Wales Personal and Social Education programme*. We provide web addresses to access information about the English, Scottish and Welsh Citizenship curricula in Chapter 8. For the rest of this chapter we will focus on the Citizenship curriculum in England, but the requirements for the provision of Citizenship Education in Scotland and Wales are not dissimilar.

Contrary to some opinions, Citizenship has a clearly defined subject knowledge content. Citizenship's knowledge is knowledge of the ways in which social, legal, economic and political institutions and systems function and how citizens may participate and be represented in the decision making of those institutions and systems; at local, national, European and global levels. It is also about developing awareness and understanding of a range of topical and often controversial issues.

Citizenship Education is about much more than 'knowing'. Young people will not enter adult life as 'active citizens', raising their 'voice' to contribute to democratic society, if they are not given opportunities to develop the skills they need to participate. Kohlberg's work on the staged development of moral reasoning, its linkage to our conceptions of justice and his argument that progression to higher stages is dependent on construction from the lower stages, illustrates the point (Kohlberg, 1968, 1984). Citizenship Education therefore aims to enable young people to research, express and justify an opinion on the issues of Citizenship and to make their opinions heard to the decision makers. Moreover, it hopes to encourage young people to go deeper, exploring and questioning the moral and philosophical basis of their views and the views of others. These skills and concepts of Citizenship are of at least equal, and actually we believe of more, importance than the subject knowledge of Citizenship.

However, what is most significant about Citizenship as a curriculum subject is not the skills, concepts or knowledge elements alone. The 2002 version of the Citizenship National Curriculum contained the following key phrase, right at the beginning of the document.

'Knowledge and understanding about becoming informed citizens is developed when applying the skills of enquiry and communication, and participation and responsible action' (QCA, 1999). In the rewritten version of the Citizenship curriculum, for implementation from September 2008, the phrase has less prominence, but has not gone away; now reading, *'Develop citizenship knowledge while using and applying citizenship skills'* (QCA, 2007). The fourth element of the Citizenship curriculum, 'curriculum opportunities', gives a sense of how this might happen in practice.

Perhaps it would be helpful to think of it this way: Citizenship knowledge, Citizenship concepts, Citizenship skills (or processes) and Citizenship opportunities are sometimes referred to as the 'strands' of Citizenship Education. We would like you to think of those strands not as distinct and lying parallel to one another, but inseparably entwined, plaited, along their length, each inextricable from the others. It is this that we believe makes Citizenship a unique and powerful curriculum subject.

Bearing this in mind, we first give more details about the separate strands of the Citizenship curriculum. In Chapter 3 we move on to discuss what their inextricable nature means for Citizenship pedagogy and the Citizenship teacher.

Citizenship processes

The National Curriculum designates a whole section to the skills or 'processes' of Citizenship. These fall into three categories, detailed in Figure 2.1: critical thinking and enquiry; advocacy and representation; and taking informed and responsible action.

Figure 2.1 Key processes of the Citizenship National Curriculum

Students should be able to:

Critical thinking and enquiry	Advocacy and representation	Taking informed and responsible action
a) Question and reflect on different ideas, opinions, assumptions, beliefs and values when exploring topical and controversial issues and problems.	a) Evaluate critically different ideas and viewpoints including those with which they do not necessarily agree.	a) Explore creative approaches to taking action on problems and issues to achieve intended purposes.

Figure 2.1 (Continued)

Critical thinking and enquiry	Advocacy and representation	Taking informed and responsible action
b) Research, plan and undertake enquiries into issues and problems, using a range of information, sources and methods.	b) Explain their viewpoint, drawing conclusions from what they have learned through research, discussion and actions, including formal debates and votes.	b) Research, initiate and plan action to address citizenship issues, working individually and with others.
c) Interpret and analyse critically the sources used, identifying different values, ideas and viewpoints and recognizing bias.	c) Present a convincing argument that takes account of, and represents, different viewpoints, to try to persuade others to think again, change or support them.	c) Negotiate, decide on and take action to try to influence others, bring about change or resist unwanted change, managing time and resources appropriately.
d) Evaluate different viewpoints, exploring connections and relationships between viewpoints and actions in different contexts (from local to global).		d) Assess critically the impact of their actions on communities and the wider world, now and in the future, and make recommendations to others for further action.
		e) Reflect on the progress they have made, evaluating what they have learned from the intended and unintended consequences of action, and the contributions of others as well as themselves.

Programme of study for Key Stage 4, QCA (2007)

Students need to be encouraged and supported to research into issues for themselves. Only by experimenting with research can the skills of research be learned: 'learning by doing'. Students will encounter a range of facts about issues, and alternative opinions (some masquerading as facts) about those issues. Students need to learn how to distinguish between fact and opinion but also to question the reliability, the validity, of the 'facts'. They need to develop skills of data interpretation, of analysis and evaluation, and to be able to argue their own point of view about an issue; a point of view based on interpretation, analysis and evaluation of (perhaps conflicting) evidence. They need eventually, as Kohlberg has suggested, to be able to argue with reference to philosophical understandings of the nature of justice and democracy. They need to develop the skills of listening to, and responding to, other points of view; not just denying views they disagree with, but engaging in reasoned debate and argument. Perhaps most crucially, students need to develop the skills to be able to take *'informed and responsible action'*; to actually have the capacity to engage with their communities (from the local to the global level) and find practical ways to improve them. Students need to develop the skills to *'take action on citizenship issues to try to influence others, bring about change or resist unwanted change, using time and resources appropriately'* (QCA, 2007).

Citizenship concepts

The National Curriculum identifies three key concepts that underpin the study of Citizenship: Democracy and Justice (for example *'weighing up what is fair and unfair in different situations'* and *'considering how democracy, justice, diversity, toleration, respect and freedom are valued by people with different beliefs, backgrounds and traditions within a changing democratic society'*); Rights and Responsibilities (for example *'investigating ways in which rights can compete and conflict, and understanding that hard decisions have to be made to try to balance these'*); and Identities and Diversity (for example *'exploring the diverse national, regional, ethnic and religious cultures, groups and communities in the UK and the connections between them'* and *'exploring community cohesion and the different forces that bring about change in communities over time'*) (QCA, 2007).

These are not exclusive categories; each links to, inextricably entwines with, the others. Indeed that is perhaps the most crucial thing to understand about Citizenship Education, that each concept, each skill, each fact is tied to others; it is the whole picture that we seek to understand.

Citizenship Education must address a range of key conceptual questions: What is 'justice'? What is 'fairness'? What is 'democracy'? Is, for example, 'first past the post' a fairer or more democratic election system than 'proportional representation'? What are our 'rights'? What are our 'responsibilities'? Who am 'I', who are 'you'? What is the importance and significance of identity and culture? All of these are far from simple issues.

The identity question is a good starting point for Citizenship Education (worth considering in your planning, see Chapter 4). Many texts on the theories of learning will advise you to start your teaching from 'the student' (see work by Vygotsky and Bruner for example (Capel *et al.*, 2005, Chapter 5). Who are they, and what do they already know? Exploring students' own identities is more complex than it might at first appear, because we all have multiple identities.

> I begin my Year 7 classes in Citizenship with identity. I get my students to make 'identity hats' decorated with images, symbols and words that say something about who they are. This often results in some very interesting exchanges between the children, and leads into discussions about stereotyping. A few years back, for example, one British Asian girl decorated her hat with a crucifix (a Christian symbol) and a wheel (a Hindu symbol). Now, in Bradford, where I teach, the general perception among many white British people is that all British Asians in the city have family heritage in Pakistan and are Muslim. True to form, one of the white boys in my class challenged the girl. *'Why do you have a cross on your hat, you're a Muslim and that's a Christian symbol?'* The girl replied *'No I'm not. My dad is originally from India, and is a Hindu. My mum is English and a Christian. Both of those are part of my identity.'*
>
> Nurgus Qadri, Head of Citizenship, Hanson School, Bradford

The former Conservative cabinet minister Norman Tebbit once posed the 'cricket test'. He questioned the loyalty and allegiance to Britain of young black men in the UK by asking, if there were a cricket match between England and the West Indies, who would they support? Tebbit's test is simplistic. The same black youngsters who in summer wear the maroon shirts of the West Indies cricket team, with Brian Lara's name on the back, in the winter months will wear white England football shirts, with Rio Ferdinand's name on the back. In Bradford, West Yorkshire, young British Asians wear green cricket shirts with Shoaib Akhtar's name on the back, and white football shirts with 'Gerrard' emblazoned. Explain all that, Norman!

Once our own identity is (at least tenuously) established, we might consider who 'others' are, we move into exploration of notions of community and society, 'us' and 'them'. Again we are in complex, and controversial, territory. Each of us is a member of multiple communities. Andy Murray, the tennis player, is regarded as a surly Scot by the Wimbledon faithful when he loses, and a gallant Brit when he wins.

Is my neighbour, with whom I share so much, my ally and friend, or my opponent? Imagine two classmates at school; one a British

Asian, from a Muslim family, one white British. Friends, who sit together in class, help each other with homework, play football after school. Now suppose one of those children has a father who is a soldier in the British army, who is sent to fight in Iraq. Suppose the other child comes from a family who believe that the war, and the continued presence of British soldiers in Iraq, is morally wrong, or even illegal: they marched in protest against the war. The views of their parents/families, their experience, will impact upon these two children, their friendship and their sense of community and belonging. And remember, it could be the British Asian child whose father is fighting for the British army in Iraq.

This easily leads to questions about the war itself: was it right or wrong? This is a question of both legality and morality, and raises issues of rights, responsibilities, national identity and citizenship. If we disagree with British involvement, do we have a right to speak out against the war, while our government supports it, and 'our boys' are out there fighting? Are there limits to those rights? At what point are we no longer legitimately exercising our democratic right to hold an opinion different to that of our government, and oppose the war, but supporting our country's 'enemies'? At what point in our opposition do we become treasonous and criminal? Do we have a responsibility, as citizens, to our nation ('my country, right or wrong') or to some 'higher' notion of morality?

These and many other issues are real and ongoing problems for our society and for our notions of democracy, equality and freedom. As a result of 9/11 and the Iraq war, some of the freedoms and human rights that have been fought for over many centuries in the UK have been eroded; our government telling us that it is necessary to restrict our freedoms for our safety. At the time we were writing this book the Conservative shadow Home Secretary, David Davis, resigned that post, and his seat in Parliament, following a narrow victory for the Labour government in the House of Commons on the issue of extending the power of the authorities to detain people without trial to 42 days. Davis argued that this measure, and others, such as proposals to oblige UK citizens to carry biometric identity cards, amounted to an attack on our civil liberties, and chose to fight a by-election to highlight these issues. What would Burke, Jefferson and Niemöller have to say to us about this?

We hope, from this one example, to show how apparently easy questions, and discussion of seemingly straightforward issues, can rapidly become contentious and controversial in Citizenship Education. Not only are such philosophical and moral questions likely to quickly arise when teaching Citizenship content (because these concepts and Citizenship knowledge are inextricably entwined), exploring and addressing them is part of what Citizenship is about. That is the challenge and the excitement of the subject.

Citizenship range and content

The 'range and content' of Citizenship Education is, if you like, the 'facts', the 'subject knowledge'. Consider how closely the list of Citizenship content in Figure 2.2 relates to the excerpt from Postman and Weingartner (1969) and Rischard's (2002) list of the twenty key problems facing the world in the twenty-first century (both in Chapter 1).

Figure 2.2 Citizenship range and content

Citizenship focuses on the political and social dimensions of living together in the UK and recognizes the influence of the historical context. Citizenship helps students make sense of the world today, and equips them for the challenges and changes facing communities in the future.

The study of Citizenship should include:

a) Political, legal and human rights and freedoms in a range of contexts from local to global.
b) The roles and operation of civil and criminal law and the justice system.
c) How laws are made and shaped by people and processes, including the work of parliament, government and the courts.
d) Actions citizens can take in democratic and electoral processes to influence decisions locally, nationally and beyond.
e) The operation of parliamentary democracy within the UK, and of other forms of government, both democratic and non-democratic, beyond the UK.
f) The development of, and struggle for, different kinds of rights and freedoms.
g) How information is used in public debate and policy formation, including information from the media, and from pressure and interest groups.
h) The impact and consequences of individual and collective actions on communities, including the work of the voluntary sector.
i) Policies and practices for sustainable development and their impact on the environment.
j) The economy in relation to citizenship, including decisions about the collection and allocation of public money.
k) The rights and responsibilities of consumers, employers and employees.

Figure 2.2 (Continued)

l) The origins and implications of diversity and the changing nature of society in the UK, including the perspectives and values that are shared or common, and the impact of migration and integration on identities, groups and communities.

m) The UK's role in the world, including in Europe, the European Union, the Commonwealth and the United Nations.

n) The challenges facing the global community, including international disagreements and conflict, and debates about inequalities, sustainability and use of the world's resources.

Programme of study for Key Stage 4, QCA (2007)

So, that's easy then. A Citizenship teacher needs to be an expert in Philosophy, Law, Politics, Economics, Sociology, Social Policy, Environmental Science, History, Human Rights, International Relations and Development Studies. No worries, we can do that!

Perhaps it is no surprise to learn that Ofsted reports (Ofsted, 2005, 2006) have criticized the failure of many schools to fully implement the Citizenship National Curriculum, and make the point that those schools who are making a 'good job' of Citizenship Education are those that have recognized the need to employ trained Citizenship specialists. Just as we, as Citizenship teachers, would not pretend to be competent to teach PE or Mathematics, there is no reason to suppose that a PE or Mathematics teacher has the background and depth of knowledge and understanding to teach Citizenship. Think about this again when you read Chapter 4 where we look at the different possibilities for a curriculum structure for Citizenship.

Citizenship teachers clearly need to have a very broadly based general, and at times in-depth, knowledge. A Citizenship teacher is a polymath. Consequently, we would hope that people coming into Citizenship Education through specialist PGCE courses, and going on to become Citizenship NQTs, have had their Citizenship subject knowledge audited during the selection process for courses, and have put in place personal development programmes for areas of identified weakness. We would hope also that teachers, who have, later in their careers, moved into Citizenship Education from other subjects, are similarly committed to the development of their own understandings. In Chapter 8 we will, however, direct you to sources of information, and more particularly to teaching resources, which will enable you to access the subject knowledge you require.

Curriculum opportunities

The fourth 'strand' of the Citizenship curriculum is the most practical, outlining the broad strokes of strategies to teach the other three strands (concepts, knowledge and skills) together (see Figure 2.3). These activities, processes and opportunities are integral to student learning and *enhance their engagement with the concepts, processes and content of the subject'* (QCA, 2007). In the next chapter, ('Practical teaching strategies'), and in Chapter 5 ('Citizenship beyond the classroom' and 'Citizenship beyond the school gates') we start to break down these broad strokes to suggest more specific teaching strategies.

Figure 2.3 Citizenship curriculum opportunities

The curriculum should provide opportunities for pupils to:

a) Debate, in groups and whole-class discussions, topical and controversial issues, including those of concern to young people.
b) Develop citizenship knowledge and understanding while using and applying citizenship skills.
c) Work individually and in groups, taking on different roles and responsibilities.
d) Participate in both school-based and community-based citizenship activities.
e) Participate in different forms of individual and collective action, including decision making and campaigning.
f) Work with a range of community partners where possible.
g) Take into account legal, moral, economic, environmental historical and social dimensions of different political problems and issues.
h) Take into account a range of contexts, such as school, local, regional, national, European, international and global, as relevant to different topics.
i) Use and interpret different media and ICT, both as sources of information and as a means of communicating ideas.
j) Make links between citizenship and work in other subjects and areas of the curriculum.

Programme of study for Key Stage 4, QCA (2007)

Post-16 Citizenship

Citizenship Education is a statutory entitlement of young people at Key Stages 3 and 4, i.e. between the ages of 11 and 16. However, it would seem somewhat perverse if we ended teaching and learning for and about democracy there: just as young people approach the age where society recognizes them as adults; as they are about to achieve a range of social and democratic rights (such as the right to vote); as they acquire a range of adult responsibilities; and as they end their juvenile status in the eyes of the criminal courts. At this stage of their lives Citizenship really becomes less abstract and theoretical, less something to be modelled and role-played, and truly something to be lived and acted upon.

From September 2008 it is possible for post-16 students to undertake an AS and A2 level course and examination in Citizenship Studies. We consider this examination in a little more detail in Chapter 7. However it will always be the case that only a minority of students will choose to do this course. All AS and A2 courses, in fact, are undertaken by larger or smaller minority groups; AQA (the examinations board that offers AS/A2 Citizenship studies) lists over 60 current AS/A2 courses on its website. Even the most popular subjects, such as English, are taken by a minority of post-16 students. This is not the route to education for democracy for all.

Opportunities for continuing and further education in Citizenship should be available for all post-16 students: whether or not they are taking an examination course in the subject; whether they are AS/A2 students, repeating GCSE or other pre-16 courses, following the new diploma (from September 2008) or other vocational education routes; and whether they study in schools, sixth form colleges or further education (FE) colleges. Indeed, opportunities for education for democracy should be extended beyond these educational institutions to reach out to those young people who leave formal education at the age of 16.

Fortunately there are many such opportunities, and a lot of work has been done to disseminate good practice in post-16 Citizenship Education, most notably by the Learning and Skills Network (LSN, see Chapter 8). LSN worked with a number of schools and colleges on 'pilot projects' for post-16 Citizenship. These projects led to the publication of a wide range of excellent teaching resources and more, all of which are available free of charge from LSN. We commend them to you; indeed you should obtain them even if you are only teaching Citizenship up to Key Stage 4, since many of the activities are easily adaptable for younger age groups.

A new Citizenship Education opportunity is provided by the reforms to 14–19 education that took effect from September 2008. As part of the new diploma routes in post-16 education, students must undertake an extended project. However all post-16 students (even those following more traditional AS/A2 courses) have the option of undertaking the project (which is a free-standing level 3 qualification and can be considered by university admissions tutors). The project needs to demonstrate students' ability to carry out a piece of research and to engage critically with their subject. Since the purpose of the project is to show both depth and breadth of understanding, the project should go beyond the narrow confines of an academic subject and show some engagement with 'real world' issues. Clearly it is possible for the project to be based around active citizenship work, which would give a rich and fruitful area of investigation.

Also from September 2008, post-16 students may undertake a post-16 baccalaureate (such as the AQA 'bacc'). The baccalaureate has at its heart a traditional AS/A2 programme. Students add to this 'broader study', which might include: developing critical thinking skills (perhaps evidenced through AS Citizenship Studies, Critical Thinking or General Studies); 'enrichment activities' (such as community work or personal development activities); and the extended project as described in the previous paragraph. The purpose of the 'bacc' is to demonstrate and recognize the all-round achievements of post-16 students, and provide a much fuller picture of their aptitudes and abilities than has ever been possible from a simple three 'A' level diet. Clearly this programme has multiple opportunities for students to pursue their understandings of Citizenship Education and education for democracy.

This book was being written just as the new post-16 programmes were being rolled out to schools by the Department for Children, Schools and Families (DCSF), the Qualifications and Curriculum Authority (QCA) and the examinations boards, and it is too early to assess their full impact on the terrain of post-16 education. However, we believe there are multiple opportunities for Citizenship Education in the new schemes, and for Citizenship PGCE students and NQTs to be at the forefront of shaping the future of post-16 education; *carpe diem!*

Finally, let us return for a moment to where we began this chapter, thinking about democracy in schools. In most schools with a sixth form, and in some sixth form colleges, there is a 'head boy' and/or 'head girl'. In many more traditional schools some members of the sixth form are selected to be 'heads of house', prefects or some similar role. It is worth questioning how these appointments are made, and what scope exists for democratizing the process, either by a vote of all the school's students, or by some kind of vetting of appointments by the school council as representatives of the students. One small step towards democracy in schools, tomorrow the moon!

Summary

Citizenship is a core National Curriculum subject. Young people are legally entitled to an 'education for democracy' in our schools at Key Stage 3 and Key Stage 4. Ofsted (2005, 2006) have reported on the progress schools are making towards meeting that entitlement. It is clear from the reports that while many schools are making excellent progress in the provision of Citizenship Education, there are many more who have only half-heartedly engaged with the National Curriculum requirements, and others who have failed to recognize their full ramifications. Ofsted have also commented that those schools that have made most progress are generally those that have appointed specialist Citizenship teachers. We know of many such teachers, graduates from Citizenship PGCE courses, who have become 'Head of Department' for Citizenship, or 'Citizenship Co-ordinator' either immediately at the end of, or within one year of completing, their NQT year. Usually these teachers have made a nuisance of themselves, pointing out to Headteachers the deficiencies of the existing Citizenship provision in their schools, until the Headteacher says *'well if you think you can do better . . .'.* We urge you to take up the challenge and 'do better'. You can find some ideas on how you might set about doing so in the rest of this book.

Teaching and learning Citizenship in schools Part 2: Pedagogy and practical teaching strategies

3

Citizenship pedagogy

In Chapter 2 we offered an introductory explanation to the key 'strands' of Citizenship: knowledge, concepts, processes and opportunities. We have also returned, a number of times, to the point that these strands are very much inseparable. But what does this mean for Citizenship teachers, in practice, for *their* skills and their pedagogy?

We have the privilege of interviewing candidates for admission to a PGCE course in Citizenship Education. Part of our interview process invites candidates to bring in an artefact that they might use as stimulus material in a Citizenship classroom and talk for about five minutes about how they would use it. After the candidates have spoken, our first follow-up question is usually along the lines of, '*What would you do next in the lesson?*' A very high proportion of candidates reply with something like '*I'd ask the young people to have a discussion about the issues.*' Candidates, responses from this point onwards really determine whether they will be offered a place on the course, as we begin a fierce interrogation about why they think '*having a discussion*' is worthwhile, and how they will manage such a discussion.

In order for young people to have worthwhile discussions (or debates) around the range of topical and controversial issues that are part and parcel of Citizenship Education, they require both high quality information about the issues, and to have developed the skills needed to engage in such discussions. We cannot assume that the skills, any more than the knowledge of particular ideas or topics, are already present; they must be taught and learned. We have seen weak teachers begin a lesson with something like '*Today we're going to have*

*a discussion about the arguments for and against foxhunting, David –
you start'*. In the ensuing ten minutes the 'discussion' consists of *'It's
cruel'*, *'no it's not'*, *'my dad says it's wrong'*, *'your dad knows nothing
about it'*, *'I think it's good'*, *'you're evil'* and so on. The discussion fails
to have any real educational benefit because (a) there is no factual
information available to the students on which to base discussion,
(b) there is no framework for management of the discussion, (c) the
students do not have the skills to discuss in any purposeful way and
(d) the discussion does not lead to any conclusion.

To be an effective teacher you must possess or develop a strong
knowledge of your own subject: the teacher is regarded by DCSF
as the *'expert within the school workforce in teaching and learning'*
(TDA, 2007). For Citizenship teachers, that means expertise not only
of the institutions and issues based content of the subject, but also of
the important Citizenship skills (including the skills of discussion/
debate, and of the opportunities the curriculum presents to develop
those skills and that knowledge).

Most crucially, Citizenship teachers must know how to teach their
subject, the most appropriate teaching methodologies. In Citizenship,
that means methods and activities that encourage learning of
both skills and understanding, that, for example, give students
opportunities to learn about their consumer rights, and question
their basis, as they develop their ability to assert them. Citizenship
teachers share an understanding that a didactic, lecturing, teaching
style is insufficient to teach their subject: that copying a table on law-
making in the UK from the book or board is not Citizenship. Instead,
their pedagogical approach could be described as active, interactive,
relevant, critical, collaborative and participative (Huddleston and
Kerr, 2006).

The aim of much of the rest of this chapter is to give practical ideas
of activities that can be used as part of your toolbox for developing
students' Citizenship skills and knowledge. They are 'shells' that
you can adapt to fit different topics. However, we believe that
Citizenship pedagogy is not simply a matter of increasing the number
of participatory and interactive games and challenges you use. We
believe it is poor Citizenship teaching that begins with, *'Today's
lesson is about how laws are made'*, even if you go on to add *'let's start
with a card-sort, move on to paired discussions and snowball into a
class debate'* (though incorporating such activities is no bad thing).
Instead, Citizenship requires a more fundamental rethink of how its
content is approached.

Where to start?

Let us remind you of a very old joke. A city dweller was driving around Norfolk in his posh car, and eventually got hopelessly lost. Seeing a local 'country bumpkin' by the side of the road he pulled up and asked how to get back to the city. The 'bumpkin' replied *'If I were you, boy, I wouldn't start from here'*.

We recognize that for the practical purposes of planning it is necessary to make lists of subject knowledge content that will be explored with students, and identify at what stage of the year and term that knowledge will be encountered (and we give an example of this in Chapter 4 on planning). However, we also believe that care needs to be taken, when adopting such an approach, not to miss the point of Citizenship Education. Starting a lesson or unit with the statement *'Today we're going to learn how local government operates'*, makes for potentially dry and inaccessible lessons, and the inevitable question from some students, *'What's the point of this?'*.

If we were you, boy (or girl), we wouldn't start from there.

In order to engage students' interest in the functioning of the system we suggest you begin by demonstrating how the system impacts upon your students' lives. Start from real world issues, local, national or global, that you believe are of real concern to the young people you are teaching. Better still, ask students to suggest the issues. These might be to do with the local community (for example local crime rates, vandalism and the safety of young people's recreation areas) or the chances of getting a job when they finish school. They might be national/international issues; for example global warming and the environment (maybe because they've recently heard something on TV or the radio).

Move from exploring students' concerns about these issues, to an exploration of who has the power to make decisions on such matters and only then how that power is exercised ('how local government operates' or 'how laws are made'). For example, your lesson plan may well be headed 'Media bias', but we would urge you to be flexible and adaptable enough to take your start from a specific news item that is current and of interest to your students (maybe even from the school newsletter!) and build your teaching around it.

Not only is such an approach more likely to engage students, it enables skills, concepts and knowledge to be closely woven together. Below, Ben Howard shares some strategies he has used to make his lessons relevant to the lives of his students.

Relevance, I remember being told as a trainee, is a fundamental of effective lesson planning. Connecting subject matter with students' own experience is essential if they are to engage with the lesson and learn. To underline the point, it is worth considering your own recent experience as a learner. How many times have you, as a PGCE student or NQT, sat through a training session and thought *'Why do I need to know this? Is this really necessary? How is this practically going to help me in the classroom?'* I know I did several times. The result being that I switched off and learned only a limited amount.

Acknowledging and recognizing the importance of relevance is easy. It is actually making your subject matter relevant that is the challenge, but it offers the ultimate reward – students engaged and learning. I think being Citizenship teachers we are in a unique position. Our programme of study is still comparatively light touch and non-prescriptive. We have the freedom to be creative and make the concepts and topics we teach tangible. I try to approach topics from an angle that offers learners a greater chance of making a connection with lessons. Effectively I try to teach required components of the programme of study by wrapping it up with content students are more likely to identify with.

Teaching a topic such as human rights can be, if you as a teacher allow it, rather disconnected from students' everyday experience. I work in a fantastic school – an all boys' sports college of comparatively modest but rapidly improving academic achievement. In my teaching I have used real life case studies involving sports and sporting role models the students can relate to. I developed lessons on Muhammad Ali as a conscientious objector, the Basil D'Oliveira affair and sporting boycott of South Africa, and Jesse Owens in the Berlin Olympics. When teaching about globalization, I created lessons on the globalization of Premier League football.

Moving away from the sports theme, other lessons I have found successful include youth curfews, child soldiers and smacking, on the human rights front; illegal downloading/music piracy in relation to the economy and consumer rights; and the possible effects of violent computer games when examining the role of the media.

In exploring some of these issues I have found the use of narratives effective. Stories that students can empathize and identify with stick in the mind long after the minutiae and staid detail, or abstract concept, is forgotten. For example, when teaching about the criminal justice system, I give pupils a number of fictional scenarios concerning young people in trouble with the law. They take on the role of judges to decide an appropriate sentence, having been given certain criteria by which to assess each case.

Ben Howard, Citizenship teacher, Carshalton Boys Sports College

Where you can, support students to use their newfound understanding to express their voice in a 'real' way, to make a change or influence those with power to do so. There is sometimes a false divide made between citizenship lessons which prepare students to take responsible action, and 'active citizenship' projects in the school and community in which students 'make a difference'. While the latter are important (see Chapter 5) the divide should not be such a stark one. Students *can* take part in individual and collective action (one of the 'curriculum opportunities') in the classroom (see Ben Hammond's account of Key Stage 3 Citizenship lessons at Deptford Green School on pp. 53–5, and Figure 5.2, pp. 81–2, 'Six steps for Citizenship projects').

Practical teaching strategies

The sections below give examples of what teaching and learning in a Citizenship classroom might actually look like. Of course, those described are purely intended as a starting point, some ideas that have worked for us. You may well be using some of the activities already, you might doubt the usefulness of others; that's the way it should be, there is no all-encompassing rule about what makes good Citizenship teaching and learning (though we hope we have given you some idea about what we think does not).

For all the activities described here, some underlying assumptions are made about the classroom environment. These relate to steps all good teachers take to create a safe and positive working atmosphere, in which students feel that they and their opinions are respected and valued. That includes removing barriers to inclusion of all students: thinking about the layout of the room; the pace of the lesson; the use of praise; the accessibility of resources; and catering for different learning styles. We come back to these issues in the section on lesson planning in Chapter 4.

Discussion

Discussion is a hugely important part of what goes on in the Citizenship classroom. It enables students to find their 'voice', to hear other viewpoints, to have their opinions questioned, and to persuade others to their point of view.

However, discussion can seem daunting. It is easy to picture either *'So what do you think?'* met with stony silence, or heated and increasingly uncontrollable students shouting out inaccurate or offensive statements. Certainly, discussions in Citizenship relating to the key concepts of justice, rights and identity will, by their very nature, be controversial. In fact, Holden defines a controversial issue even more broadly, as anywhere there are conflicting values, opinions and priorities (Holden, 2007). So that's pretty much every issue with teenagers then!

Setting ground rules and sticking to timings can help. But, according to Holden, the key *'is to give structured and focused tasks so that the lesson does not become either a free-for-all "slanging match" nor a series of aimless discussions, where there is danger that prejudices are reinforced and ignorance debates with ignorance'* (Holden, 2007). We include a range of ideas for structuring discussion over the next few pages, from questioning to role play. These should be used alongside opportunities to research the topic under discussion – the 'curriculum opportunity' to use and interpret different media and ICT comes into its own here. Students need to be able give an evidence base for their opinion, not just 'shout the loudest'. The reflection or debrief where the lesson is drawn together, is also crucial. It is easy to run out of time and cut it short, and students are left without a chance to reflect on and take forward what they have learned.

In order for discussions to be constructive students need boundaries or rules to work within. One of the first activities I do with a new class is to set ground rules for our lessons. First we discuss what rules are and why they are important, i.e. for conducting constructive debates and discussions, to create boundaries in order to make students feel at ease and be able to contribute.

I ask one student to volunteer to act as scribe, to stand up in front of the class and write the rules on the board. Students call out their ideas and if the rest of the class is in agreement they are added to the list. It is important that they agree on them and that none of their rules conflict with school rules. Being able to create their own ground rules gives students ownership of the lesson and makes them more likely to participate in discussions.

Some helpful ground rules that are chosen by most classes:

- Give everyone an opportunity to speak
- Do not make fun of other people's opinions (a really important one that nearly every class I have taught has listed)

Each student copies the rules into their exercise books so they can refer to them. I also display a copy of the rules in the classroom, which provides students with a constant reminder and enables me to refer to the rules when necessary. These rules then form the basis of any classroom discussions. Students are more likely to want to contribute in lessons if they have had a say in how those discussions will take place.

(Continued)

Although the students create the rules I do not let them include anything that will break the school rules, e.g. we can talk on our mobile phones during lessons; we can drink and eat during lessons, etc. Usually I have one student who argues that this is not fair, that if I have the final say over the rules why should they bother suggesting any, why don't I write them all? I argue that all societies work within rules or laws and within our school we are just a microcosm of wider society, so it is vital that we learn to abide by rules too.

Alero King, Humanities, Citizenship and Sociology teacher, Queens Park Community School, Brent

Questioning

Some element of discussion, through questions from student to teacher and teacher to student, is a constant of teaching. Questioning can be a very powerful tool, particularly when it is 'stepped' (each question represents a manageable chunk of a larger whole) and all students are given the chance to take part by first working, individually or in groups, on the answer or stimulus material.

'Why' is probably the most powerful question we can ask, and once someone provides an answer, asking 'why' again is the best way to encourage the development of a line of argument. One of our favourite Citizenship lessons is 'Labels in our clothes', a lesson about global Citizenship issues (you can find this lesson on the 'Just Business' website, see Chapter 8). The lesson begins by asking students to examine the labels in their clothes (inside shirt collars, in waistbands of skirts and trousers, inside shoes), to see if they can discover where their clothes were made. In itself this is a simple research task – Citizenship skills in action. Gathering together students' responses invariably produces a list of countries, the majority of which are in the 'Third World' (or if you prefer, 'countries of the South', or 'less developed countries'; even the language you use is potentially controversial and open to debate in Citizenship). Now the question, 'Why?' Why, when we are capable of making all the garments we are wearing here in the UK, are we buying our clothes and shoes from Thailand, Malaysia, Sri Lanka, China, Indonesia and so on? Depending on the age and existing knowledge of your students (and we've successfully used this activity with everyone from Key Stage 2 to postgraduate students), the answers you receive will be more sophisticated or less sophisticated, but the responses are likely to include: *'they can make them cheaper'*; *'cheap labour'*; *'child labour'*. Now ask 'why' again. Why can they make them cheaper? Why is labour cheap? Answers may include *'fewer rules and regulations about health and safety, the environment', 'high levels of unemployment so people are desperate for work'.* Now ask 'why' again. Why are there fewer rules, why is there unemployment? The process should never end, and leads to deeper and deeper levels of understanding. Now go and read your textbooks on theories of learning again, and look at the ideas of Vygotsky and his 'zones of proximal development' and 'scaffolding'.

Start small and snowball

If you start a discussion from cold, posing 'big' questions to the whole class, you may get no answer at all or only engage those students who are both confident to speak out and have also started to form their opinions. Starting small and getting bigger is a good way to get students thinking and talking.

So start students on their own, or in pairs, providing a focused stimulus material if you can: ask students to respond to a specific image, quotation or statement, or complete the ranking activity described below. Give them a set amount of time, a specific question and a specific format for recording their views. For example, *'you have five minutes to discuss and write down (on this post-it/mini-whiteboard/flip-chart sheet) whether you would agree or disagree with a proposal to ban supermarkets from giving out plastic bags to customers, and three reasons for your answer.'*

Pairs can be 'snowballed' into fours and then even eights, joining with another pair to exchange views, or you can move directly to full class discussion.

Group work can be difficult to manage when you first start teaching, but is a 'curriculum opportunity'. So starting with pair work and building up to bigger groups can also be a useful way of developing your skills, as well as those of students.

Ranking

An example of stimulus material which, in our experience, provides lots of food for thought (and discussion) is ranking. For example, ask students to rank their human rights according to which they think are most important and which are least important. Ranking nine cards using a diamond shape provides more nuance in the ranking (see Figure 3.1). The best discussion comes when, as in this example, there is no clear answer.

Figure 3.1 How would you rank your rights?

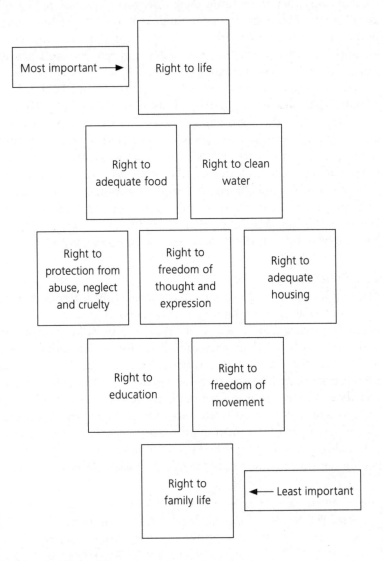

Stand on the line

Getting students to demonstrate their opinion physically means they all have to think about their view, even those who are reticent to express it orally. Move desks to give enough space for students to stand along one side of the classroom. Read or project a statement such as 'Young people who commit crimes should be harshly punished'. Ask a few students, or all the class, to stand along an imaginary line (we call this a 'values continuum line') running from 'strongly agree' at one side of the room to 'strongly disagree' at the other, with 'neither agree nor disagree' right in the middle. Ask some students why they're standing there. *'Because Dan did'*, or *'I don't know'* are not acceptable answers. Emphasize that as they hear their peers' opinions, they are free to change their opinions and move along the line, but when they move they may have to explain why; whose arguments have convinced them?

Brian Jacobs, a Citizenship teacher at Cedar Mount High School in Manchester, has an interesting variation on this activity. He asks students to write their opinions on paper, and hangs a washing line across the classroom. Students are issued with clothes pegs and invited to hang their opinions on the line. The washing line can then remain in place for the next few lessons, and as students' understandings and opinions develop and change, as a topic is explored in more depth, they are invited to edit and/or move their opinion along the line. We think this has some interesting possibilities for assessment work; have a look at the contribution of Aashiya Chaus in Chapter 7.

Circle-time

Making changes to the environment can make a big difference to how students feel about contributing to discussion. The classic example is moving chairs from rows, where they may be talking to others' backs, into a circle, where they can all see each other and they are not hidden behind their desks. As with all discussion, setting ground rules is important. The advantage of moving is to change the context and allow different forms of interaction, but that means you have to be clear about what is expected. Ideas for managing the discussion include having an object (microphone, ball or whatever) that you have to be holding in order to speak. If you want to say something you have got to keep your hand up until the object is passed to you.

Facilitating classroom discussions is very important: steering the discussion and drawing conclusions ensures that a few pupils do not dominate and that focus is maintained. Depending on the group and the issue under discussion, I approach the role of facilitator in different ways.

As a teacher, you have to be very careful about stating your own opinions because you are in a very powerful position and pupils can be easily influenced. Playing the role of a neutral chair can be best. This is the role I tend to play; I briefly introduce the topic, make a few points for and against the issue and then ask the pupils what they think. However, if there are no responses I will make 'devil's advocate' statements that I know will be controversial just to get them going.

(Continued)

   If you are having a discussion on an issue about which you feel strongly it is sometimes difficult not to say what you think. When this happens I tend to start discussions by explaining how I feel about an issue and why; I try to use an example about myself, or someone I know to make it more real and interesting.

   All students are entitled to their own opinions; however that does not mean they can be offensive towards others. When pupils make a racist, sexist or homophobic comment it is very important to challenge it and explain why it is not acceptable. Often pupils repeat things they have heard without realizing the implications of what they have said.

Alero King, Humanities, Citizenship and Sociology teacher, Queens Park
Community School, Brent

Formal debates

Formal debates provide a clear structure for how discussion will proceed. Set a clear motion, or statement ('This class believes that the UK should adopt the Euro'), and give time for students to research and structure an argument for or against. It is normal debating procedure to have two or three speakers on each side. In classroom terms this could mean overall six groups of two or three students. Each group either nominates a speaker or gives their speech together, starting with a group that is in favour of the motion, and proceeding alternately, working to strict timings. It can help to ask each group to research and write on a particular argument or angle, to avoid too much repetition in the debate. A final two groups could be given the task of an overall summary of each set of arguments, to be delivered at the end. Or non-speaking 'audience' members could be asked to come up with a specified number of questions that they will ask when the debate is opened to the floor. They will need to decide who they want to address their question or query to, and the speakers will need to be prepared to respond. At the end, take a vote to see what 'this class believes'.

   Another approach to debating, sometimes called a 'cotton bud' or 'paper clip' debate, which gives each participant a clear number of opportunities for participation, is described below by Emily Miller, a Citizenship teacher at North Manchester High School for Girls.

Debating and sharing ideas are central to Citizenship. Some students find this easy, and have the confidence to speak in front of their peers. Others, however, find this a real challenge, despite often having many good ideas worthy of sharing. How can you get the best out of *all* your students? One format I have used to try to address these differences is 'the paperclip debate'. In this activity, students sit in a circle and each have three paperclips. You introduce the discussion and elicit initial thoughts and questions. A good topic for this could be a current issue, such as the proposal to reduce the voting age to 16. The rules are that during the course of the debate every student *has* to make a point or comment – each worth a paperclip. Those who have more to say can use all three (make three points), but no more. As the teacher you can prompt the debate by making provocative statements or directing questions at particular students. At the end you can feedback using the 'what-went-well-and-even-better-if' model and encourage students to engage in self-reflection.

Emily Miller, Citizenship teacher with TeachFirst,
North Manchester High School for Girls

We have witnessed an example of this activity taking place where one vocal student had run out of paperclips. Her neighbour, who really wanted to hear the rest of what she had to say, offered her one of his own so that she could continue speaking. The teacher was flexible enough with the rules of the activity to allow this to happen; rules are to help not to hinder.

Role play and drama

Well designed role play is a particularly powerful tool in citizenship education. It can ensure that every viewpoint in debates about complex controversial issues is considered. Careful allocation of players to roles can ensure that students are obliged to express opinions that are not their own, and can help to develop skills of empathy. A single role play can encompass local and global, as well as political, legal, social and moral dimensions of a debate. Role play can encourage thinking about the ways to resolve conflicts, and how individuals and groups can act to bring about change.

Fairbrass, in Ofsted (2006)

Not only all of this, but role play can also help put across facts about procedures or structures far more effectively than simply reading about them or writing them down. For example, when you come to explore with students how Parliament functions, don't bore them to tears with an interminable lecture about the various stages a bill goes through before it becomes an act; rearrange your classroom to look like the House of Commons, with benches down each side, and a Speaker's Chair. Ask some students to play the role of Prime Minister, Home Secretary and so on, others to play the role of their counterparts in opposition, another to play the Speaker and some to play the clerks and more. Role play a debate in Parliament about issue(s) your students are concerned about.

The Citizenship Foundation can provide you with a free guidance pack for running a mock Parliament, and they run regional and national mock Parliament competitions that your school can take part in. (They also produce role play materials for mock trials, and you can enter your students for regional and national competitions in this area too.) There are many other commercially available, or free, published role play activities that are suitable for use in a Citizenship classroom. Global Citizenship issues are particularly well served by role play activities produced by the development education networks; your local Development Education Centre (DEC) can provide examples such as 'The Chocolate Game' (Leeds DEC) or 'The Paper Bag Game' (Christian Aid). We would also recommend 'Timber', 'The Debt Game' and 'The Tourism Game', all on the 'Just Business' website. On a larger scale, there are opportunities for young people to participate in mock United Nations General Assemblies or Security Council debates. See Chapter 8 for the relevant contact details.

However, with a bit of imagination, you can design your own role play activities around current issues, providing as much or as little predetermined information on their roles as your group needs. Below, Ben Miskell describes a role play that he and his peers on a PGCE course created, about an LEA meeting on school food. He gave his class roles as representatives from different groups: parents, students, catering staff, a pressure group and the manufacturers of turkey twizzlers! Ben's account is also a great illustration of the power of approaching Citizenship learning through issues relevant to students.

When I was a PGCE student at the University Centre at Bradford College, training to be a Citizenship teacher, my fellow students and I were invited by our tutor, as part of our coursework, to design a role play that would explore issues of democracy around a topical issue that would be of interest to a Key Stage 3 class. At the time, the government had recently responded to Jamie Oliver's healthy food campaign by requiring school kitchens to revamp their menus to replace chips and 'turkey twizzlers' with salads and fresh vegetables. The popular press, and TV news, had shown pictures of mothers arriving at school gates at lunchtime and pushing takeaway burgers, kebabs and chips though the railings to their children, who were rejecting the new menus.

This seemed to us to be a perfect opportunity to explore Citizenship issues, because the government's new policy seemed profoundly undemocratic in that the people directly affected, the schoolchildren, were not consulted about a decision about their own diet. This was a live issue with the children we were meeting on our school placements, who felt (rightly in our opinion) that this was not fair. Our role play imagined a meeting of the local education authority to make a decision about school catering, with representatives of the children, their parents, an imaginary 'healthy food' pressure group, the manufacturers of 'turkey twizzlers' (protesting how nutritious their products were), the school's catering staff and more. The debate explored the case for a healthy diet, the constraints on schools' catering budgets, the children's right to choose what they ate and many more issues. As a follow-up we explored how children might make their views known to the school's management through school council, letters to the Headteacher, and 'direct action', such as boycotting school meals.

Ben Miskell, Citizenship teacher,
Alder Community High School, Tameside

We have a particular view of role play; for it to be truly effective, everybody in the room must be in, and remain in, role; and that includes you, the teacher. If not, the illusion is instantly broken. Some published role play games have written into them a role for you, but if there is no such role, write your own, as a government official, a UN observer or something similar. Try to resist the urge to jump in, out of role, and tell 'little Jonny' off if he is misbehaving. Rather, go and speak to him in your role and ask him some questions that he should answer in his role to re-engage him. We have also worked with classroom assistants, for example, and enlisted them as 'journalists'. We've asked them to look out for students who are not engaged, or who are finding the activity difficult, and to go to interview them in role to help them find a way back into the game. There are many other possibilities. Good role play should stimulate your students' imaginations, but don't forget your 'inner child'; use yours as well.

The use of drama does not have to be limited to different formats of debate. Ian Kirby (2006) suggests a range of ways in which drama can be used to spark and structure discussions. For example, the teacher can take on a character themselves, with students preparing questions to ask them (sometimes called hot seating). The 'Forum Theatre' technique, originally used in the early 1970s by Augusto Boal, involves a group acting out a situation illustrating a dilemma or problem. After watching the drama once, the audience are encouraged to 'freeze' frame the drama and explain what they think the characters should do differently. Alternatively, after 'freezing', one or more of the characters could be asked to give their internal thoughts at this point in the drama.

A word of caution. Young people can get really carried away in drama based activities, really taking on board and 'becoming' their characters. Emotions can run high and fierce arguments break out. It is important that you allow time at the end of the activity for people to come 'out of role'. We recommend taking off any costumes, handing back 'character cards' and moving seats, to sit next to different people. You should also 'debrief' the activity; have a discussion about the issues that were raised, out of role. Make sure any remaining tensions are dealt with before your students leave your room. We have heard of fights breaking out in corridors after role play lessons, with students still in role!

Group work

You have already read about the importance of group work to discussion, whether that is completing a diamond-nine ranking in pairs, or role playing a trial in a group. However, we think group work is worth a separate mention, as a 'curriculum opportunity' (students must *'work individually and in groups, taking on different roles and responsibilities'* (QCA, 2007)) and significant feature of Citizenship pedagogy. Below, Harsharan Tung, a Citizenship teacher at Belle Vue High School for Girls, underlines the value of group work in her account of facilitating such work during her PGCE placements.

Students' profiles at my two PGCE placement schools were quite distinct, and certainly brought home the complexities of group work. During my first placement, group work was an integral part of my teaching and the experience demonstrated the value of group work to Citizenship lessons. One lesson that stood out for me was a Year 7 local government lesson which involved the students enacting a council meeting to decide how to spend their funding. The children were completely engaged with their roles as members of the community and the council. Having the roles allowed all students to contribute, thus tackling a common problem faced during group work. I also allowed the students to decide among themselves which roles they would like to play and to elect their chairperson, therefore introducing the democratic process of making decisions right from the start. I was amazed during the debrief, when the children were giving virtually textbook answers to my questions, indicating how beneficial well-planned and structured group work can be. The students gained knowledge and understanding about the democratic process, local council meetings and local finance, and at the same time developed their skills of communication, participation and responsible action. This proved to be an exemplary Citizenship lesson, and one consequently borrowed by my Head of Department and used for an Ofsted inspection.

Riding on this success I went into my second placement with lessons incorporating pair work and group work and faced a rude awakening on my very first lesson. The starter involved students working in pairs where one had to talk about anything they wanted for one minute while the other pretended not to listen. Out of 16 pairs only one pair played the part, the rest either just sat there chatting away to each other or did not speak at all. Similarly, group discussions were impossible as students possessed poor listening skills and were, in the main, not familiar with active learning strategies. Consequently, discussions and debates were constantly disrupted with students speaking over each other and proving difficult to manage. It was tempting, I must admit, during the second placement, to avoid group work like the proverbial plague!

However, I persevered and one strategy I used was to make the lessons as relevant as possible to all students. For example, during a lesson on the economy students were put into groups, given various roles within a company making bids to form a Dream Pop Band (variation of a Dream Football Team) in order to engage the interest of the girls too. Being given a budget and bidding for their favourite singing artists proved much more alluring than dealing with simple goods and services. More importantly, introducing the element of competition and team work helped groups to gel, as collaboration and effective communication became paramount. Rules had to be adhered to or monetary fines were imposed ensuring that instructions were followed.

(Continued)

My first placement gave me a goal to work towards, my second placement helped me realize the difficulties involved and develop strategies to tackle them. As a PGCE student you are limited in terms of 'ownership' of the class, so short-term strategies need to be adapted. As an NQT you can then use that experience to begin embedding the essential skills required for group work from day one, and witness the improvement.

Harsharan Tung, Citizenship teacher,
Belle Vue High School for Girls, Bradford

Obviously, its very nature means that discussion is an important element of group work, and this is partly where its merits lie. However, pair work or small-group work does not have to be reserved for debate or other discussion based activities. Working in a group to carry out research or plan a course of action can help build a range of skills including the ability to explore and negotiate courses of action; manage time; listen to the views of others; express an opinion; and reflect on participating. Such actions can range from completing a research worksheet using the internet, to organizing a paper-recycling scheme at school (see Chapter 5 for more on Citizenship projects at school and community level and Andy Thorpe's account of developing the quality of group work through peer assessment, pp. 109–11).

There are many other examples of group work activities that could be adapted for the Citizenship classroom in Robert Chambers' book *Participatory Workshops* (2002). Chambers is an academic and practitioner in the field of international development. Over many years he worked with poor rural communities in Africa and elsewhere to enable them to develop and express their hopes and aspirations for the development of their communities, and to turn these into real actions (Citizenship Education, in fact, is what Chambers was doing, though he might not have used the term). Along the way Chambers gathered and developed a whole host of 'participative methodologies', for initiating discussions, for developing debates and for deciding on and managing practical courses of action. We recommend the book to you.

Incidentally, Chambers began his career in Kenya as an administrator. We thought this quotation from the introduction to the book might amuse you:

> For those in administrative services around the world who are incompetent there are four main trajectories: out of the service; exile to a remote posting where harm done will be less noticeable; into an evaluation unit; or transfer to train others . . .I had already done a spell in a remote posting where the damage I did, although serious, was localized (I have been back to apologize) . . . So, I was consigned to be a trainer. . . To George Bernard Shaw's 'He who can, does. He who cannot, teaches' can be added 'he who cannot teach administers' and finally 'he who cannot administer, teaches administrators'.
>
> Chambers (2002)

We've heard another version of this that says *'he who cannot teach writes books to tell other people how to teach.'* We couldn't possibly comment!

Student participation in assessment

Assessment should be an integral part of teaching, and as such should be as active and participatory as other elements of a Citizenship lesson. We won't say any more here, because this topic is covered more thoroughly in Chapter 7, 'Assessment in Citizenship'.

Finally, a note on writing skills

In all the focus on participatory, active Citizenship lessons, it can be easy for written tasks to be overlooked. Ofsted (2005) note that *'in some schools, pupils produce very little written work in citizenship, and some files contain work that is low level, including much completion of worksheets. This work is too often well below the pupils achievement in other subjects, and higher attainers tend to be the group least well served by these activities.'* They remind teachers that the subject does have a written requirement and that students should be given opportunities to explore topics in depth in writing.

In contrast to discussion or activity based tasks, students can view writing as *'boring'* or complain that *'this is not what Citizenship is about'*. Weaving written tasks into lessons, so that they form an integral part of an activity (such as writing a speech for a debate) or have a 'real' context (such as writing the text for a campaigning website), can motivate students. Examples based on activities in this chapter might include students writing why they chose a certain position on the physical values continuum, or writing a newspaper report as a 'journalist' present at a mock Parliamentary debate.

Some students find writing difficult, and simply being told to 'write an essay on fairtrade' is hard for everyone. The clearer, more specific instructions you can give students about what and how they should write, the better the results will be. One good way to do this is to use writing frames, such as the one in Figure 3.2, which help students organize their thoughts and understand the 'aim' of each paragraph or section.

Figure 3.2 Writing frame

Essay: The voting age should be lowered to 16

Length: 2–3 sides of A4, handwritten   **Date due:**

Useful sources of information
➤ p. 42 in your textbook
➤ The worksheet you completed in the ICT room
➤ Your notes from group discussion.

Introduction
➤ Keep this section short
➤ Explain that there are arguments both for and against this statement, and that you are going to write about both

---

Arguments for
➤ Try and give at least three arguments for lowering the voting age
➤ Spend at least three sentences on each, really explaining the argument
➤ If you can, back up the argument with facts and figures

Arguments against
➤ Try and give at least three arguments against lowering the voting age
➤ Spend at least three sentences on each, really explaining the argument
➤ If you can, back up the argument with facts and figures

Conclusion
➤ This is very similar to the introduction
➤ Sum up, saying that there are arguments on both sides
➤ Give YOUR opinion, with one or two reasons that you think are the most convincing

Summary

The range of teaching strategies we have outlined require you to have teaching skills of the very highest order. It is difficult to manage role play and other group work in the classroom, especially if the school has no tradition of working in this way (see Harsharan Tung's experience above). It is inevitable that you will have failures when you first try to use these approaches to teaching and learning. You can minimize those failures while you are training to teach by sharing your ideas about what you want to do with your PGCE mentor and host teachers, and enlist their help in practically managing the activities; even their presence can make class management issues easier. Start with simple tasks, and build up to the more complex ones as your confidence grows.

If and when it goes wrong, take some time out and then try to analyse and reflect; was it all a disaster or was it going smoothly until . . . ? What could you modify next time to make it work better? Try, try and try again. Even the very best teachers, with many years of experience, have the occasional bad lesson. Don't beat yourself up, learn from the experience and move on. We promise you, when these activities do work (and they will, we've tried and tested them all over many years in all kinds of schools, with all kinds of students), you will experience the most rewarding of teaching experiences, and your students will learn and remember.

Just as we believe young people learn the skills of democracy by practising, so we believe new Citizenship teachers must learn the skills of the democratic classroom through actively trying to create that classroom.

Planning for Citizenship

4

There is an old aphorism that 'failing to plan is planning to fail'. This is certainly apt in teaching – that Friday afternoon Year 9 lesson you thought you could 'wing' is there to remind you. Consequently, planning is a huge part, and a hugely important part, of what teachers do. Broadly speaking, planning takes place at three levels:

- Short term: Lesson plans
- Medium term: Units or modules
- Long term: Scheme of work

In this chapter we explore each of these levels, highlighting issues for you to be aware of and reflect on, and practical approaches for you to consider. To illustrate how each level of planning informs the next, on the path from National Curriculum to individual lesson plan, we have provided some concrete examples of planning documents. To begin with, though, some general points about planning, applicable to any subject.

First, as your peer trainees or NQTs compare how late into the night they have been planning, or the colour-coordinated flashiness of their latest interactive whiteboard resource, it is easy to get sucked into thinking that 'length of time spent' or 'number of smiley faces and stars added' directly correlates to quality of planning. Good planning does not have to mean fancy. Beautiful multi-coloured worksheets or all-singing plenaries certainly have their place, but they are not all there is to a well-planned lesson. At its heart, planning is about knowing where you are going: what the purpose of every activity, lesson or unit of work is and how it contributes to students' skills and understanding. Your first priority is to be clear in your own mind what your end goals are, and to create a path to those goals.

The path that you take with one class will never be exactly the same with a different class, or the following year. As the National Curriculum, exam specifications or school curricula change so do your end goals, and as the needs of the class and of individual students vary, so does the exact path you take to those goals. So the second point we want to emphasize is that planning is not a one-off event, a few hours spent developing a scheme of work or a series of lessons that we roll out year on year. Good planning involves constant reflection: what worked well in that lesson and what didn't; what approach might suit this particular group of students; how can I tie-in this topical issue into this module; what would I do differently next time? Constant evaluation and reflection on the success of your lessons and the needs of your students means that you will be constantly modifying and improving your plans.

Finally, in the past, certainly when we were at school, there was a tendency to see content planning, and planning for behaviour, as two separate strands of the preparation teachers do. So on the one hand deciding what should be taught when, and on the other how to control 'pupils' when they start 'messing around'. The idea that a student's behaviour is unrelated to the content of the lesson, and can be considered separately, is no longer pedagogically credible. The onus is no longer on students to avoid distraction when they are bored and confused, but on teachers to provide an environment and activities which enable students to engage and learn. The Every Child Matters and differentiation agendas (see Chapter 6 and below, respectively) reinforce this point, as does Citizenship, with its focus on student-led, participatory teaching and learning. Seen in this light, good planning is reflecting and preparing to get the best out of students in all respects.

Long-term Citizenship planning

There is no legal requirement that Citizenship is incorporated in the school curriculum in a set way. However, most schools are adopting one of, or a mixture of, four approaches:

- Designated Citizenship lessons
- Cross-curricular through other subjects
- 'Form time' and assemblies
- Collapsed timetable events

How Citizenship teaching is structured at your school will have a big impact on all the planning that you do, at all levels. There are pros and cons to each approach, described more fully below. Kerr *et al.* (2007) argue that the success of a school's Citizenship programme is determined less by the way it is structured and more by having a small dedicated team, strong and clear leadership, and up-to-date resources. Ofsted agrees that most important is a *'strong and identifiable core programme, irrespective of how it is delivered'* (Ofsted, 2005). However, we would argue that providing such a programme, one that is coherent and supports student progression, is difficult if Citizenship is only taught through other subjects and the odd assembly or event. It is also important to bear in mind that all students are entitled to Citizenship Education. Lunchtime activities for the motivated or community based work for the less motivated may work well, but such enrichment activities for small groups do not constitute Citizenship provision for all students. Of particular concern are schools that claim to 'deliver Citizenship through the school ethos', without specifying what they are actually doing. Ofsted would agree that for some such schools *'the judgement of "unsatisfactory" came as a surprise because key staff took the view that the school was developing "good citizens" in the broadest sense. This is not the issue. The National Curriculum provides a programme of study for citizenship. This is additional to any general provision that supports pupils' development as young citizens, whether in the ethos of the school or the implicit contribution made by other subjects'* (Ofsted, 2005).

A study carried out by the National Foundation for Education Research, and published by the Department for Education and Skills (DfES, now the DCSF), asked students their views on different ways of teaching Citizenship. *'Students report that the best form of delivery is as a discrete element of the curriculum'* (Kerr *et al.*, 2007). We would agree and strongly advocate at least a 'core' of designated Citizenship lessons. But don't take our, or even Ofsted's or students' words for it, once again we'd encourage you to be reflective about what you think works and doesn't work. Below, Ben Hammond, Citizenship Co-ordinator at Deptford Green School, does just that.

My first real experience of Citizenship at Deptford Green (an inner-city secondary school in the south-east of London), was at the beginning of my second PGCE placement. I followed a Year 7 class on a 'Citizenship morning' – three continuous off-timetable lessons from morning through until lunch – and what I saw and experienced changed the way I taught and thought about Citizenship Education.

I followed 7VE on their local area 'safety on the streets' investigation: from the classroom in lesson one (using local area maps and photos as a means for discussing key issues and problems); to a tour of identified local community 'hotspots' (with students' recording, justifying and evaluating their safety concerns and solutions); and then to a computer suite in lesson three, where students captured and consolidated their

(Continued)

learning by working in small groups to make presentations for local council officers. All this in an energetic, fun and positive learning environment created by teacher and students alike. As with the students, I was hooked, and returned to the final weeks of my first PGCE placement with renewed focus on what Citizenship is all about: learning experiences that start with applied investigation and action for change, not dry, abstract knowledge. 'Question + Action x Skills x Knowledge = Change.'

However, joining the school the next year, I realized that this ideal, and the Citizenship mornings in which it played out, wasn't all smooth sailing. Enabling genuine student choice means this is no 'off-the-shelf' curricular model; schemes are constantly rewritten; planning for progression is tricky; and the extent to which Citizenship has equal status with more established subjects through this model could be questioned.

In response, in my second year at the school, we trialled discrete one-hour Citizenship lessons for Years 7 and 8. In the main, an hour a week still allowed us to remain true to our pedagogic principles: when a young student was hurt in a road accident near the school, our school council worked with us to develop a Road Safety Investigation unit for her year group, with students surveying the dangerous junction in question and presenting their findings and solutions to executive members of our borough council. When students voted a nearby underpass as the most unsafe location around the school, a year later they worked hand in hand with the council and urban designers to secure half a million pounds of funding for its wholesale community-led regeneration – all through the regular, timetabled lessons.

Yet, the hour a week presented us with inescapable difficulties. Local community trips were more limited. Planning became less a shared endeavour. Our emphasis on students taking action for change was restricted. Citizenship began to morph into the hour-a-week straitjacket: losing spark, energy and application.

Fast forward to the present and I have just taught the first Citizenship morning of the term at Deptford Green. This time around we have tried to mitigate some of the drawbacks of this approach through some concrete steps: increasing the number of mornings through the year (from six to nine); creating ongoing student portfolios to exemplify work, progress and achievement; and inviting teachers from all other subject areas to take part.

It is exciting and energizing to be involved in the mornings again. The year ahead features more local area investigations: film-making for Boris Johnson; photo stories for the Young Mayor of Lewisham; collaboration with young people from a fairtrade co-operative in Ghana; and work with the Council on their recycling initiatives.

(Continued)

The mornings are affirmed and consolidated by the new secondary National Curriculum. They are a reminder of what Citizenship Education is and should be: engaging, real life, applied and community focused. Welcome back.

Ben Hammond, Citizenship Co-ordinator, Deptford Green School

Designated lessons

A core of designated Citizenship lessons provides a regular and irremovable opportunity for Citizenship learning, and helps ensure that all elements of the curriculum are covered, not just those that fit in easily with other subjects. It allows a school to employ specific, trained, Citizenship teachers, familiar with both the content and pedagogy of Citizenship, rather than leaving it to untrained and sometimes unwilling members of other departments. Providing timetable time can help indicate to staff and students the importance of the subject, and ensures that the aims and purposes of Citizenship, as a distinct subject, are not confused with the aims of other subjects.

Of course, there are possible problems with designated lessons. Kerr *et al.* (2007) suggest that they may encourage more traditional teaching and assessment practices or limit the flexibility to respond to current and topical events as they arise. As you might have guessed from reading Chapter 3, we wouldn't agree this has to be the case.

Citizenship taught in Citizenship lessons needs to be ordered in some way, and again there are no rules about how this is done. A common option is to create 'themes' or 'units' along the lines of content, providing opportunities for the development of Citizenship knowledge and skills across them all. It is up to each school to make judgements about the relative 'weight' of each strand of the content element of the Citizenship curriculum, and how they are combined into units of work. In Figure 4.1 you can see one possible approach, the bare outlines of one school's Citizenship scheme of work. What do you think are the benefits and drawbacks of this arrangement of the curriculum? At this point, we would refer you back to the section 'Where to start?' (in Chapter 3) to consider how you approach the content of such units.

Figure 4.1 A Citizenship scheme of work

	Year 7	Year 8	Year 9	Year 10	Year 11
Term 1	Identity and diversity	The Media	Young people and the law	Democracy and being British	Global Citizenship
Term 2	The school community	National government	Human rights	The EU	The UN
Term 3	Local government	Fairtrade	The role of voluntary groups	Money	Conflict and conflict resolution

Cross-curricular Citizenship

Knowledge and skills cannot be neatly 'cookie cut' into clear subject areas (in Chapter 6 we discuss further the issue of whether the curriculum should be divided along such artificial boundaries). There are some subjects with strong links to Citizenship, and it can be helpful for students to see these links, as well as finding Citizenship time in a pressured timetable. Common subjects for teaching aspects of the Citizenship curriculum include Geography, History, Religious Education (RE), Science and Personal, Social, Health and Economics education (PSHEE). Which subjects each school chooses, and which topics within those subjects, is up to them. Figure 4.2 offers some suggestions.

Obviously, the more subjects and topics Citizenship is taught through, the more fragmented it will become. In fact, Citizenship became a mandatory subject in 2002 because, in its previous incarnation as a cross-curricular strand, it was not having the desired results. To help maintain Citizenship's coherence and identity, students should always know that they are studying Citizenship (and teachers that they are teaching it): it should be indicated in units of work and articulated to classes. In addition, the relationship between Citizenship knowledge and Citizenship skills (see Chapter 2) means that the pedagogy, as well as the content, of Citizenship must spread to other subjects in which it is taught. Copying notes on the pros and cons of genetic screening is probably not Citizenship learning, while a debate on this issue could be. As Ofsted puts it *'enquiry in science and participation in sport, meritorious as they are in their own right, are not about National Curriculum citizenship, unless they are dealing with material from the citizenship programme of study'* (Ofsted, 2005).

Figure 4.2 Opportunities for teaching Citizenship through other subjects

Subject	Citizenship questions
Geography	• What might local people think about a proposed housing development and what actions could they take to express their views? • What impact does the use of resources have on the environment, for example the relationship between fossil fuels and global warming? What individual and national strategies could help tackle the problem?
History	• What are the differences between the authoritarian Nazi government and our government in the UK today? • What are the differences between medieval justice and the justice system today?
Science	• Is it acceptable to use human embryos for research? • Would you be happy to buy GM products? • How should the government plan to ensure our energy supply in the future?
Religious Education	• What views do different religions hold on charitable donation – is it the responsibility of a citizen? • How does the media portray religion? • Do students have the right to wear religious symbols in school?
English	• What Citizenship themes are illustrated in our texts (e.g. nature of government in *Animal Farm*)? • Can you use the strategies of persuasive writing you have learned to persuade someone with the power to make a change? • In what ways are these advertisements effective?
ICT	• What value would you put on these different internet sources of information on a topical issue? • Do you trust these crime statistics? • Can you create a presentation or send an email to inform or persuade an audience on an issue you think is important?
Maths	• How much interest would you pay in actual terms on different types of loans? • Based on the number of votes, who would win this election, using different electoral systems?

Figure 4.2 does not mention PSHE – this is because we thought it deserved a special mention. It is a common mistake to 'lump' Citizenship and PSHE together. Personal, Social and Health Education (which has more recently become Personal, Social, Health and Economics education), pre-dates Citizenship in the curricula of most schools. PSHE has never had a statutory presence in schools: under the National Curriculum, 'guidance' has been published about what PSHE should consist of, but the government stopped short of making PSHE a legal requirement per se. However, many schools have failed to recognize the difference between its standing in the curriculum and that of Citizenship. Indeed, many schools have failed to even recognize the significant differences between Citizenship and PSHE in terms of content.

PSHE is about personal, private choices, and students' interaction with others at a social level. Citizenship is about individuals as members of society, and their rights and responsibilities. *'Thus conflict resolution in citizenship is not about the problems experienced in individual parent–teenager relationships. However, topics like bullying, teenage pregnancy and drug abuse, which are naturally the content of PSHE, take on a citizenship dimension when the questions addressed are to do with topical local and national issues, policy, and what can be done to bring about change'* (Ofsted, 2005).

Where, despite these differences, Citizenship and PSHE have been linked together in programmes called PSHCE or similar, the Citizenship curriculum is often diluted (Ofsted, 2006).

Form time and assemblies

Form time can be a good forum for exploring school-level Citizenship activities like school councils or other student-consultation processes, to discuss current issues in the news and in students' lives and for the logistics of 'active citizenship' projects in the school or wider community. Assemblies can be a time to use outside speakers, and to celebrate achievement in Citizenship. However, there are administrative and logistical demands on both form time and assemblies (notices to be given, planners to be signed, uniforms to be checked). So these slots do not generally provide enough time in which to reliably teach significant chunks of the Citizenship curriculum. In addition, form tutors may not have training, expertise or even willingness to teach the subject. As such we think these spaces are best viewed as opportunities for Citizenship enrichment activities, rather than Citizenship entitlement.

Collapsed timetable events

'Make a Difference Day', 'Earth Day', 'Unity in Diversity Day', 'Election Day': just some of the options for Citizenship events, which can be motivating and fun. They can provide opportunities for all students, not just a few, to 'take informed and responsible action' and get involved with the wider community. There are outside organizations and individuals who may be able to contribute to the day, from prison warders to volunteer groups – for more ideas, see Chapter 8.

At Nower Hill we have an annual Citizenship Day for each of Years 8–10 to complement their weekly Citizenship lesson. Students attend six workshops run by outside speakers from charities, the police, politicians or by staff members who want to engage students on a Citizenship issue that they care about. In recent years sessions have included NatWest Bank on personal finance, Compassion In World Farming on intensive battery farming, teachers giving sessions on body image and the media and the Romance Academy taking sessions on healthy relationships. A group called Project Illusions sent a professional magician to inspire students to 'Go Change the World'.

The days have been going for about five years now and have been incredibly well received by students. They like to see that teachers they don't normally associate with the Citizenship department are actually really active citizens, getting out there and campaigning just as the students do for their Citizenship Studies GCSE coursework.

Students also enjoy working on 'real life' projects to improve their community – we have had artwork produced by students on one Citizenship Day used by the police's Operation Blunt across London, and as a result of regularly having speakers from St Luke's Hospice, we have become the school that raises the most money for them each year. Several students have been inspired to volunteer, campaign or arrange fundraising events for causes they have heard about on Citizenship Days. It has also helped them understand some of the career options available in the public and voluntary sectors.

The day takes a lot of work to organize: ensuring materials are provided (paper, pens and presentation facilities); arranging refreshments for everyone involved; coordinating older students to take speakers around; and re-rooming other lessons. We arrange cover for form tutors who go to each session with their class. This helps them later discuss the issues raised on the day with their form, and also means speakers do not have to handle any behaviour problems. Another element of planning is vetting the speakers in advance (to check that they will give an engaging and interactive session, and not just a lecture), and having a back-up plan in case any drop out at the last minute.

It is hard work, but incredibly worthwhile as students come to their next Citizenship lessons energized and inspired to focus on the subject!

Lucy Morgan, Teacher in Charge of Citizenship GCSE, and Jon Mason,
Head of Citizenship, Nower Hill High School, Harrow

Medium-term Citizenship planning

Medium-term planning takes different forms in different schools, but normally means units of work or modules that make up the scheme of work for the year or Key Stage. Some Citizenship teachers find that their Head of Department will provide them with comprehensive and well-resourced units of work, describing sequences of lessons, others that they have to write their own. Here are some key questions to consider when constructing or evaluating a unit of work:

- Has the subject matter been translated into key aims (broad questions or areas of study)?
- Are key aims sequenced in a logical way?
- How does the unit fit into the scheme of work or course requirements?
- Is there a range of activities and resources suggested, adaptable for different groups and different individuals?
- Are the proposed activities accessible, engaging, relevant to students' lives, and varied in terms of learning styles?
- Are opportunities for assessment included?

In Figure 4.1 you saw one example of a Citizenship scheme of work, the Citizenship curriculum arranged in 'units' across Key Stages 3 and 4. This skeleton scheme of work simply indicates the title of each unit and when it is studied. Over the next few pages, in Figure 4.3, you will see one of these unit titles – 'Year 8, Fairtrade' – developed into a unit of work. Andy Thorpe, Citizenship teacher at Bradford Academy, wrote this unit, and has kindly agreed to allow us to share it here. Andy is an outstanding teacher, but that is not to say we think this is the only way to structure and present a unit of work. In terms of content, too, this is just one approach other teachers might look to give students greater opportunity to critically analyse fair trade. We offer this unit of work as an example, to illustrate what medium-term planning can look like.

Short-term Citizenship planning

Much time during PGCE and early teaching years is spent constructing lesson plans. So whether you trained to teach Citizenship or another subject, you will no doubt be well acquainted with lesson planning techniques, and the now generally accepted three-part format: starter, main activity, plenary. We are not going to go over all of this again, but in Figure 4.4, on p. 70, we have included some key questions to help you reflect on and refresh your lesson planning for Citizenship – worth thinking about both before and after lessons. We would also like to refer you back to the Chapter 3 sections on Citizenship pedagogy, and practical teaching strategies. In Figure 4.5, on p. 72, you will find an example of a lesson plan. This is Andy

Thorpe's lesson plan for lesson 2 of the Fairtrade unit of work in Figure 4.3 ('Inequalities of international trade'). Again, this is not the only way to present a lesson plan, and certainly not the only way to teach about trade. It is simply an example, though we think a strong one, of the end point of the planning progression from National Curriculum to individual lesson. First though, we would like to mention two 'buzzwords' in planning.

Differentiation

All children are different, with different experiences, achievements and talents. Differentiated teaching involves responding to these differences. It means adapting your interaction, instructions, resources and support to the needs of individual students, rather than teaching to a single homogenized block of students. Differentiation does not, therefore, just mean 'making the worksheet easier for the less able kids' – such categorization is not helpful. It means making constant judgements about your class, group, individual student and resources.

There will be some students who have had their needs formally identified and assessed, and your school should have a Special Educational Needs (SEN) department who can offer you advice on how you can support these students. Other students may be part of Gifted and Talented programmes, and you should receive advice on how to stretch and challenge them. However, you need to think about the needs of all the students in your class and what you can do to help them engage and learn. Of course, this can seem an impossible task when you have a class of 30, and a large part of your energy is expended keeping five of them on their seats. Plus, you can't teach in a way that suits all the students all the time. However, you can plan to regularly use a range of different approaches to learning, varying your teaching style to enable different students to engage. Howard Gardner's 'multiple intelligences' (e.g. Gardner, 2006), and the simpler VAK (Visual, Auditory and Kinaesthetic) model of learning styles are good ways to start thinking about the different ways people learn.

The good news is that Citizenship teaching and differentiated teaching can have a lot in common: good Citizenship teaching and differentiated learning are inherently student-led. Citizenship offers opportunities to value a range of skills and intelligences that are not always valued in other subjects. Citizenship teaching also puts an emphasis on encouraging students to reflect on, and take responsibility for, their own individualized learning, and on active participation in lessons.

Figure 4.3 A unit of work: Year 8, Fairtrade

Year: 8

Theme: <u>FAIRTRADE</u> (Links to new NC – 1.1b, 1.2a, 2.1a, 2.2b, 2.2c, 2.3a, 2.3b, 2.3c, 2.3c, 2.3d, 3e, 4a, 4b, 4c, 4d, 4e, 4f, 4g, 4h, 4i, 4j)

Aims and objectives:	Knowledge and understanding:		Key skill development:
• To introduce the concept of Fairtrade • To consider the need to be a responsible consumer • To highlight current understanding on Fairtrade and ethical consumerism	Starter: Main: Development: Plenary:	Introduce the theme by agreeing with the class a separate definition of the terms 'fair' and 'trade'. Brainstorm on the IWB (interactive whiteboard). Put them together and define FAIRTRADE What has FT got to do with me? As consumers, do we need to be responsible? If so, think of ways in which we can be responsible. Class considers this in pairs, followed by brief feedback on the IWB Students complete the traffic light progress sheet ('before' section only) to highlight current understanding about Fairtrade Power point presentation introducing the origins of Fairtrade. Follow with a timed competitive individual quiz (FT related prize!) Revisit LOs (learning objectives), key terms and concepts	<u>Independent learners</u> • Considering new concepts and terms and expressing opinions <u>Team players</u> • Working with a partner to provide information requested by the teacher <u>Effective participation</u> • Listening to the views of others whilst gathering requested information
• To enable students to practise their role play skills • To understand the inequalities of the banana supply chain • To link different Fairtrade products to their country of origin	Starter: Main: Development: Plenary:	Revisit learning from last lesson – 'pass the pen' exercise on the IWB (student-led brainstorm) In groups of 4–5, students play the 'banana split game' which follows the journey a banana makes from grower to consumer. This highlights the inequalities in the chain and prompts students to consider a fairer approach to trade 'Where do Fairtrade products come from?' activity on the IWB – students are challenged to link a range of FT products to their country of origin (Link to Geography) Oral Q & A recap on understanding of the issues raised over the last 2 lessons	<u>Team players</u> • Working together on a group exercise <u>Effective participation</u> • Fulfilling a role in a group and also listening to and respecting the work of other groups <u>Creative thinking</u> • To come up with solutions to problems relating to international trade

Opportunities for participation:	Differentiation:	Assessment opportunities:	Resources:	Homework opportunities:
• Students are encouraged to participate in oral debate and offer ideas and thoughts (individually and in pairs)	• Quiz following power point is graded with questions of varying difficulty	• Fairtrade quiz – informal and fun assessment	• Power point presentation on Fair Trade • IWB based FT quiz	
• Planning and performing group work • Contributing to review of learning	• Groups mixed ability • Kinaesthetic activity on the IWB particularly suitable for EAL students	• Informal teacher assessment of group work	• Banana Split game • IWB FT products	

Figure 4.3 (Continued)

Year: 8

Theme: <u>FAIRTRADE</u> (Links to new NC – 1.1b, 1.2a, 2.1a, 2.2b, 2.2c, 2.3a, 2.3b, 2.3c, 2.3c, 2.3d, 3e, 4a, 4b, 4c, 4d, 4e, 4f, 4g, 4h, 4i, 4j)

Aims and objectives:	Knowledge and understanding:		Key skill development:
• To introduce the concept of active citizenship • To consider the school as 'active' member of the local community • To see active citizenship in action	Starter:	Introduce the concept of active citizenship. Compare the actions and attitudes of 'active' and 'passive' citizens in relation to community participation. Elicit examples of how one can be an active citizen. Link to how the school can be active in the community	<u>Independent learners</u> • Considering new information and showing understanding by answering comprehension questions
	Main:	Show part 1 of 'My Big Fairtrade Adventure' (22 mins). Students complete basic Q & A sheet during the programme Run through the answers and discuss the film	<u>Effective participation</u> • Listening to the views of others whilst gathering requested information
	Extension:	'The cost of Football' – IWB game highlighting exploitation in the production of footballs	
	Plenary:	Revisit LOs	
• To further develop knowledge of Fairtrade and ethical consumerism • To introduce the concept of 'Fairtrade' school status and the Year 8 challenge	Starter:	Revisit learning from last lesson – reminder of where we got up to with the film	<u>Independent learners</u> • Considering new information and showing understanding by answering comprehension questions
	Main:	Show part 2 of 'My Big Fairtrade Adventure' (24 mins). Students complete basic Q & A sheet during the programme Run through the answers and discuss the film	<u>Team players</u> • Working together on a group exercise
	Development:	Students consider the following in groups (producing a mind map). What are the causes that a school could get involved in? What things could the school community do to support/promote these causes?	<u>Effective participation</u> • Fulfilling a role in a group and also listening to and respecting the work of other groups
	Plenary:	Introduce the challenge – starting next lesson	

Opportunities for participation:	Differentiation:	Assessment opportunities:	Resources:	Homework opportunities:
• Students are encouraged to participate in oral debate and offer ideas and thoughts	• Frequent checks on understanding during and after the film	• Informal teacher assessment of understanding following showing of the film	• 'My Big Fairtrade Adventure' DVD • IWB based FT quiz	
• Planning and performing group work • Contributing to review of learning	• Groups mixed ability	• Informal teacher assessment of group work	• 'My Big Fairtrade Adventure' DVD	

Figure 4.3 (Continued)

Year: 8

Theme: <u>FAIRTRADE</u> (Links to new NC – 1.1b, 1.2a, 2.1a, 2.2b, 2.2c, 2.3a, 2.3b, 2.3c, 2.3c, 2.3d, 3e, 4a, 4b, 4c, 4d, 4e, 4f, 4g, 4h, 4i, 4j)

Aims and objectives:	Knowledge and understanding:		Key skill development:
• To explain in detail the FT challenge and the school's goal to gain FT status • To give students the opportunity to assign roles in their group, consider the challenge and then report back to the class the main aspects	Starter:	Consolidate learning using 'pass the ball' – students answer quick questions and pass the ball on to another student to answer	<u>Creative thinkers</u> • Dividing roles within the group in line with considered strength
	Main:	Divide students into their groups. Explain the challenge using the challenge sheet: A. Produce a poster promoting Fairtrade to others (students/teachers/parents) B. Produce a PowerPoint presentation describing what Fairtrade is and why it is important to the school community C. Produce a Fairtrade policy for school D. Come up with an enterprise activity to raise awareness (and money) within the school/community E. Produce a report pack that shows what you have done	<u>Self-managers</u> • Manage time, tasks and resources <u>Independent learners</u> • Consider tasks and work on their own initiative <u>Effective participation</u> • Listening to the views of others whilst researching and completing tasks
	Development:	Groups divide roles within group and work on the challenge	• Reporting back progress
	Plenary:	The 'reporter' from each group reports back the progress made by their group and what they will concentrate on next	
• To work independently on the challenge • To report back on progress and priorities for further work	**Over the next four weeks students work on the challenge with their groups. There may be an opportunity to do some joint work/ presentations with Year 7 students who are also studying Fairtrade**		<u>Creative thinkers</u> • Dividing roles within the group in line with considered strength
	Starter:	Reporters from each group give a brief update of what they have done and plan to do in the lesson	<u>Self-managers</u> • Manage time, tasks and resources
	Main:	Students work on the challenge	<u>Independent learners</u> • Consider tasks and work on their own initiative
	Plenary:	The 'reporter' from each group reports back the progress made by their group and what they will concentrate on next	<u>Effective participation</u> • Listening to the views of others whilst researching and completing tasks • Reporting back progress

Opportunities for participation:	Differentiation:	Assessment opportunities:	Resources:	Homework opportunities:
• Students are encouraged to participate in Q & A session • Students share ideas and thoughts • Students work together in small groups	• Groups are mixed in terms of abilities	• Student self-assessment of work carried out in the lesson • Informal teacher assessment of how well students are working in their groups	• Laptops • Challenge sheet • Teacher-produced 'how to...' tips sheets on each element of the challenge • Poster materials	• Gathering resources for the challenge • Working on the challenge
• Students are encouraged to participate in Q & A session • Students share ideas and thoughts • Students work together in small groups	• Groups are mixed in terms of abilities	• Student self-assessment of work carried out in the lesson • Informal teacher assessment of how well students are working in their groups	• Laptops • Challenge sheet • Teacher-produced 'how to...' tips sheets on each element of the challenge • Poster materials	• Gathering resources for the challenge • Working on the challenge

Figure 4.3 (Continued)

Year: 8

Theme: <u>FAIRTRADE</u> (Links to new NC – 1.1b, 1.2a, 2.1a, 2.2b, 2.2c, 2.3a, 2.3b, 2.3c, 2.3c, 2.3d, 3e, 4a, 4b, 4c, 4d, 4e, 4f, 4g, 4h, 4i, 4j)

Aims and objectives:	Knowledge and understanding:	Key skill development:
• To allow students to practise their presentation and peer assessment skills • To give students the opportunity to see active citizenship in action!	**Over the next 2 lessons, students present their work to each other. There may also be opportunities to present to other staff and year groups/assemblies** Starter: Students organize themselves for the presentations (poster/PowerPoint/policy and enterprise activity) Main: Students carry out their presentations and peer assessment Plenary: Students vote for the best policy/enterprise activities to be recommended for adoption by the school	<u>Creative thinkers</u> • Dividing roles within the group in line with considered strength <u>Self-managers</u> • Manage time, tasks and resources <u>Independent learners</u> • Consider tasks and work on their own initiative <u>Effective participation</u> • Listening to the views of others whilst researching and completing tasks • Reporting back progress
• To allow students the chance to practise their organization and self-assessment skills • To emphasize how the challenge fits into the bigger picture of Fairtrade status for the school	**Over the next two lessons, students complete their report packs, self-assessment sheets and end of unit traffic light progress sheets** Starter: Reminder of requirements from each student to complete the challenge successfully Main: Students work on their report packs and self-assessments Plenary: Revisit the overall objectives of the unit and talk about the continued process for achieving Fairtrade status for the school **Note: There may be an opportunity to get an external speaker to talk about Bradford's Fairtrade City status or someone from another school in Bradford which has already achieved the FT school status**	<u>Creative thinkers</u> • Dividing roles within the group in line with considered strength <u>Self-managers</u> • Manage time, tasks and resources <u>Independent learners</u> • Consider tasks and work on their own initiative <u>Effective participation</u> • Listening to the views of others whilst researching and completing tasks • Reporting back progress

Opportunities for participation:	Differentiation:	Assessment opportunities:	Resources:	Homework opportunities:
• Students are encouraged to participate in Q & A session • Students share ideas and thoughts • Students work together in small groups	• Groups are mixed in terms of abilities	• Student peer assessment of work carried out over the course of the challenge	• Work produced during the challenge • Computer/IWB	
• Students work together and independently to complete their report packs	• Groups are mixed in terms of abilities	• Student self-assessment of work carried out in the lesson • Formal teacher assessment of report packs	• Work produced during the challenge • Self-assessment sheets • Traffic light progress sheets	

ICT

Flashy ICT does not a good teacher make: the skill is in identifying when ICT can enhance learning. However, using and interpreting different media and ICT *'both as sources of information and as a means of communicating ideas'* is one of the learning opportunities for Citizenship specified in the National Curriculum (QCA, 2007). Not only that, but technology and the media is a cross-curriculum dimension. On a practical level, it is difficult to provide students with high-quality opportunities to research topical issues or discuss the influence of the media without reference to and use of ICT, whether that is internet sites, recordings of the local news or YouTube video clips. ICT is also a strong medium through which students can express their views, raise awareness and lobby, for example through emails, online notice boards and even writing a 'blog' or designing their own website.

Figure 4.4 Reflecting on your lesson plan

- What is the aim or focus of the lesson?
  This is a broad question or area such as 'How would our proposed "bill" that battery chicken farming be banned, become a law?' To establish a relevant aim, have you thought about:
  o Why it is important for students to learn this lesson?
  o How does it relate to what they already know?
  o How will you link to the next lesson?
- What are the learning objectives of the lesson?
  These are more specific statements about what students will learn, for example, 'Students should: understand the role of the House of Commons, House of Lords and the Queen in the passing of a bill to a law; know the layout of the House of Commons; understand the structure of a Parliamentary debate; be able to express a view on the strengths and weaknesses of this system.'
- What are the anticipated outcomes of the lesson?
  Outcomes are what you can measure among students to show that the objectives have been met. So for example: 'Students will be able to: draw a diagram of the layout of the House of Commons; play the role of an MP in a parliamentary debate; give one reason they think this is a good process for creating laws, and one problem with the system.'
- Have you shared the objectives or outcomes of the lesson with the class?

Figure 4.4 (Continued)

- Is your starter crisp and engaging?
- Have you thought about how to keep 'teacher talk' clear and relevant?
- Have you varied your teaching style to cater for different learning styles (visual, auditory, kinaesthetic)?
- Have you thought about how long you will give students for each part of the lesson, and is this realistic?
- How are you going to manage questioning and feedback from activities?
- Will all students be able to access and get something from each activity?
- Will everyone be challenged?
- Have you included opportunities for student participation (see the section on 'practical teaching strategies' in Chapter 3)?
- How can you maximize the likelihood that everyone participates in the lesson?
- How will you ensure transitions between activities are smooth?
- Have you made links to any topical real-life issues and to students' experience? (see 'Where to start?', p. 33)
- How will you tell if students have learned/what methods of assessment will you use (see Chapter 7)?
- What opportunities are there for students to reflect on what and how they have learned?
- Have you identified the resources that you will need for the lesson?
- How will you draw the lesson together and link it to future lessons?
- Would you enjoy the lesson?

Summary

Planning can seem to take a lot of time, particularly in the early years of teaching: we have all burnt the midnight oil at some point, desperately preparing for 8.4's 9 a.m. lesson. The good news is that good planning and good Citizenship teaching have a lot in common and your pedagogical approach as a Citizenship teacher will help you plan well. This chapter has given you some pointers to help you reflect on your own planning, and also on the larger-scale Citizenship planning of your department and school.

Figure 4.5 A lesson plan: Year 8, the inequalities of international trade

Bradford Academy			LESSON PLAN
Module: Fairtrade 2. 'Inequalities of international trade'	**Year/Stage:** 8 (L1 & R2)	**Date:** 15 & 17/04/08	**Teacher:** Mr A. Thorpe

Reflect and Connect (link to prior learning)
This lesson links to previous lesson which introduced the concept of Fairtrade
Relationship to NC Programme of Study: 1.1b, 1.2a, 2.1a, 2.2b, 2.2c, 2.3a, 2.3b, 2.3c, 2.3c,
2.3d, 3e, 4a, 4b, 4c, 4d, 4e, 4f, 4g, 4h, 4i, 4j

Resources: Banana split game, IWB activity

Learning outcomes
- Highlight the inequalities in the banana supply chain (most) and give two reasons for this (some)
- Link at least three Fairtrade products to their country of origin (all)

Lesson structure	Time
Register taken and Outcomes on the board – pupils requested to copy these into their books	**10 mins**
Starter: Revisit learning from last lesson – 'pass the pen exercise' on the IWB (pupil-led brainstorm)	**10 mins**
Main: In groups of four to five, pupils play the 'banana split' game which follows the journey a banana makes from grower to consumer. This highlights the inequalities in the chain and prompts pupils to consider a fairer approach to trade.	**25 mins**
Development: Where do Fairtrade products come from? Activity on the IWB challenging students to link a range of FT products to their country of origin (link to Geography)	**10 mins**
Plenary: Sum up main points and return to the learning objectives	**5 mins**
Extension: Students complete the traffic light progress sheet ('before' section only) to highlight current understanding about Fairtrade	

Learning styles covered:	Key vocabulary: chain, plantation, importer,
Auditory – Oral Q & A during starter, main exercise Kinaesthetic – game Visual – IWB activity	inequality

Assessment for learning processes
Discussion – starter and main activity
Justifying personal opinions – main
Plenary – to review what our learning outcomes should have been and whether we met them in the lesson

Links to Citizenship and enterprise
Lesson part of the Citizenship SOL on Fairtrade
Lesson involved group work, justifying opinion and stating an opinion that is not necessarily one's own

Reflect and connect
The next lesson will examine a real life example of active Citizenship

Homework: Look out for FT products in shops they visit	**Comments:**

Citizenship beyond the classroom

Learning never stops at the classroom door. This certainly holds true for Citizenship, perhaps more so than for any other subject. The curriculum itself points to participation in *'school based and community based citizenship activities'* (QCA, 2007). Not only is it statutory, action beyond the classroom is important logistically. A 45-minute lesson slot is not necessarily suitable for organizing an awareness-raising concert, or carrying out research in the local community. Trainee teachers are usually urged to 'get involved in the life of the school' during their training, and there is no better opportunity than helping to organize a Citizenship event 'beyond the classroom'.

There is also a pedagogical reason why thinking about Citizenship outside the classroom is important, one of consistency of message. Young people are quick to identify hypocrisy. In the Citizenship classroom they learn about the importance of action, community involvement, respect for diversity and of listening to others. They will quickly view these as irrelevant to their lives if, inside or outside the classroom, adults show little interest in these values. It works the other way too – increased participation of students in the life of schools has been shown to have a positive impact on issues such as exclusion rates and student motivation.

Despite this, the 'participation and responsible action' strand of the curriculum is often neglected in schools: *'most schools create opportunities for some pupils, but in National Curriculum citizenship this should be an entitlement for all'* (Ofsted, 2005).

This chapter aims to outline some ways in which young people can experience Citizenship at a whole-school level and in the wider community – though our list is not exhaustive. While, for practical purposes, we have a separate chapter for these activities, such a clear distinction between what goes on inside and outside the classroom is not helpful: whole-school actions (such as school council elections, or paper-recycling schemes) will have a greater impact if they are reflected on in lesson time; whole-school policies set the tone for students' experiences in the classroom; and, as described in Chapter 3, we believe that there are opportunities for both participatory learning and 'real' responsible action in lessons.

Because of this important relationship between Citizenship learning inside and outside the classroom, Citizenship teachers will invariably get involved beyond the hours they teach. When you do, it is worth bearing a couple of things in mind. First, it is not just the activity you are running that is important, but how you run it. Hart's well-known ladder of participation can be a good framework for thinking about this (Hart, 1992). At the bottom of the eight-rung ladder, young people's involvement in an activity is manipulated, decorative or just a token gesture. Hart does not view these bottom three rungs as participation at all. As the ladder is climbed young people are participating more, progressively being informed, consulted and sharing in decision making on adult-led projects. On the top two rungs young people lead and initiate action, ultimately sharing decision making with adults so that they are empowered but benefiting from adult expertise and experience.

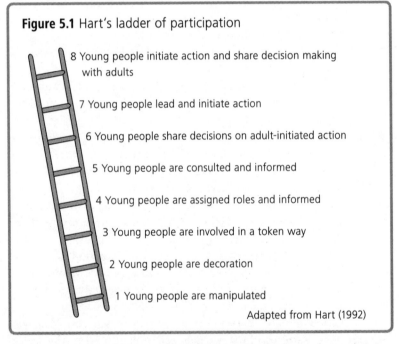

Figure 5.1 Hart's ladder of participation

8 Young people initiate action and share decision making with adults

7 Young people lead and initiate action

6 Young people share decisions on adult-initiated action

5 Young people are consulted and informed

4 Young people are assigned roles and informed

3 Young people are involved in a token way

2 Young people are decoration

1 Young people are manipulated

Adapted from Hart (1992)

The degree to which young people participate in the projects you run, or how far up the ladder they are, has a huge impact on the extent to which students develop their Citizenship skills. A slot on reception duty, which might include stuffing envelopes or opening doors for visitors, is likely to fall near the bottom of the ladder. Teacher-picked student council representatives, limited to talking about the state of the toilets, are not going to learn much about democracy. Even involvement in an all-singing, all-dancing fundraising event may fall near the bottom of the ladder if students are not involved in the planning and do not understand why they are doing what they're doing. Whatever the activity, if it is to contribute to young people becoming informed, critical, engaged citizens, the focus must be on the process as much as the action itself. If students are encouraged to *'research and evaluate underlying problems, if they take part in decisions on what can be done and how, and if they reflect on the progress they have made, personally and for their communities, they can learn as active citizens'* (Brown, 2008). Because it is the process not the action itself that is crucial, not every act of Citizenship has to be big or long term – this can be helpful to remember in schools, where you are invariably short on time and/or resources. However, that is no reason not to be ambitious from time to time. Below is an example of an inter-school project where decision making was devolved to students. What step of Hart's ladder would you put this Global Citizenship day on?

A few years ago the Council for Education in World Citizenship (CEWC) worked with a group of schools in Aylesbury to run a Global Citizenship Day for sixth form students. From the very outset the students themselves were involved in the decision making. CEWC did a brief presentation in each of three schools at a sixth form assembly, asking the students if they wanted to participate, and inviting each of the sixth forms to elect a small number of students to join a planning committee. The committee subsequently met and made recommendations about the themes that the day would address (globalization, 'third world debt', sustainability, the arms trade, poverty, famine and more), the structure of the day and the nature of the activities during the day. These ideas were then taken back to each school for ratification by a vote of the students. The students decided that they wanted a keynote speaker to introduce the day, a number of 'experts' that they could discuss issues with and a number of participatory workshops that the students themselves would run, but which the 'experts' would attend to answer questions in a plenary session. CEWC used its knowledge of the territory to provide the students with a list of possible 'experts', pointing the students in the direction of books and articles these people had written, and online biographies. The students selected from CEWC's list the names of the people they wanted (though CEWC also advised the students that if they had their own ideas about whom they would like to invite they were free to do so) and wrote letters of invitation to those people to participate. Students organized the location of the event (choosing the school that had the best facilities of the three participating), the logistics of the day, the catering and the budget.

(Continued)

This event not only provided these students with a wealth of information about global citizenship issues, but enabled them to practise and develop a wide range of Citizenship skills.

Stephen Fairbrass, one of the 'experts' the students contacted to speak on the day

To get you thinking about how participatory your, or your school's, Citizenship projects and democratic structures are, and how they could be more so, Figure 5.2 outlines six steps or stages in the process of 'responsible action'. We have suggested some possible issues and questions you and your students might want to be considering at each stage of the research, planning, execution and reflection. We are not suggesting that at every step, and for all initiatives, students will able to participate at the very top of Hart's ladder. For example, in some of the approaches to 'active citizenship' we discuss later in this chapter, such as schools councils or student consultations, the format or the issue may be predetermined. However, Ben Hammond describes below a school council the very structure of which has been student-determined, and in the same way we would encourage you to think about what you *can* do to make the process more participatory. Where you can't, it is a good idea to flag this up to students, making it clear what the extent of their role will be. Students quickly pick up if nothing ever comes out of their suggestions at school council meetings, or if they are invited to participate in the selection process for a member of staff but no one asks for their feedback once they have shown the candidates around the school.

You will see that the sixth step in Figure 5.2 involves students reflecting on the process and the action they have taken. This final step is easily forgotten, but without it the learning cycle is incomplete. The curriculum includes the requirement that students '*assess critically the impact of their actions on communities and the wider world*' and '*reflect on the progress they have made, evaluating what they have learnt from the intended and unintended consequences of action, and the contributions of others as well as themselves*' (QCA, 2007). It is good practice to evaluate the impact of any project, and students learn from being involved in the process.

Citizenship beyond the classroom

Student councils

School councils are structured and run differently in different schools. Some are made up of representatives elected or selected from year councils; others have members elected directly to the whole-school council. There may be sub-committees whose job it is to carry out different tasks or research different issues (such as bullying, teaching and learning, and catering). Some school councils meet once a week, others once a term and they vary in the level of power and budget they hold. What they *should* all have in common is an opportunity for young people to contribute to decision making at school, although it is probably fair to say that many school councils do not really enable this in a meaningful way.

However, we hear (and not just in urban myth) of school councils which genuinely do access and act on students' views about issues as widely ranging as anti-racist policies, parents' evening and teaching methods. Ben Hammond, Citizenship Co-ordinator at Deptford Green School in London, talks below about his positive experiences of the school council there. Such school councils are not only examples of high-runged participation, but also help meet Article 12 of the UN Convention of the Rights of the Child. This states that children have a right to express their views on matters of concern to them, and to have those views taken seriously.

There is much advice available on how to set up a genuinely participatory student council, and School Councils UK is a good place to start. The issue of a budget at the disposal of a student council is worth consideration for a moment. No school, no business, no government department, no non-governmental organization, indeed no household has an entirely free choice about their decisions. One of the most significant constraints to action is affordability – have we got the money to do this? Most Headteachers would probably agree that if they had double their present budgets, and could employ twice as many teachers, their schools would provide even better educational opportunities to their students. Headteachers must work within their budgetary constraints. This is an important lesson also for young people. Having a wish list is fine, but in the end they have to choose from that list what they can afford: giving a student council a defined budget each year sharpens minds considerably.

Even if you are not directly involved in the school council (many councils have a teacher representative who attends meetings instead or as well as the Headteacher), or in the logistics of elections (organizing voter registers or counting votes), as a classroom teacher or form tutor you still have a part to play. Students standing for election may come to you for advice on how the system works, what the post would involve and how to construct a manifesto or address the electorate at a hustings. Voters benefit from discussion about who they might vote for and why. Once in office, councillors may want help, and definitely need time, to representatively collect the views of their electorate and to report back the decisions and changes made by the council.

Taking time to discuss the council with students not only helps them get the most out of the system, but also shows them that the council is taken seriously schoolwide. Bringing the school council into Citizenship lessons can help with subject knowledge too: students have experience of an electoral process with which to compare systems at local, national and European levels.

Early on in its development as a specialist Citizenship school, Deptford Green realized that to ensure students develop a sense of agency at local, national and global levels they must have a real voice in their learning environments, from the classroom, through the whole school and beyond. Hence our focus on Citizenship 'culture', with school council as a flagship pathway to achieve this.

The school worked hard to establish a representative, well-supported and effective change-making school council, which students believed in and which made clear, explicit contributions to learning in classrooms, the skill-sets of students and Deptford Green's environment. The model was simple: reps discussed issues with their class and represented these in year councils (week 1), took their priorities for action to a whole-school council of two reps per year group (week 2) and then presented ideas and solutions for change to the school's senior leadership team (week 3), who worked with students to discuss and implement agreed changes, which were then fed back to classes through reps. It worked: student-led improvements included drinking water in lessons, new bicycle racks, new classroom designs, improved toilets, and specialist student teams researching learning in lessons. The list is ongoing, with over 75% of the student body voting in elections year on year and the school council held as a model to guide other schools.

To achieve this, it took much: prioritizing from senior management (with a team of teachers with school council built into their timetable, and an explicit commitment to taking students' views seriously); a transparent structure and clear administrative systems; support from the wider school (with regular staff trainings); and heavy emphasis put on school council training and evaluation. Yet there remained challenges: how to involve students in *making* change and not just simply demanding it; how to ensure continuity year on year; how to balance access to the senior leadership team with their need to build working

(Continued)

relationships with students over the longer term; how to ensure school council is an effective channel for all students' voices, and not just some.

It has been in light of these questions that Deptford Green has begun to remodel its school council, attempting to combine past successes with new solutions through:

- Evaluation – the Citizenship team, Senior Leadership Team, students and school council undertook a detailed analysis of how to take things forward: through an internet survey, focus groups and meetings.
- Ideas and inspiration – with key issues identified, we mapped what else was out there in terms of school councils (locally, nationally and globally) and students presented their ideas to the Senior Leadership Team. Drawing on the pioneering work of The Blue School, Somerset, we settled on a form of school council based not on year council meetings but on issue-based action teams. Students join teams focused on the issue they most want to improve (be it learning, student–teacher relationships or school grounds).
- Training – Deptford Green staff attended a three-day training of the 'Learning to Lead' programme that lies behind The Blue School's Community Council.
- Leadership – once briefed and clear on what it would take to implement change, as Citizenship Co-ordinator I drew up a timetable to do so, in discussion with our Director of Specialism, responsible for student voice.
- Commitment – but it took more than a plan to make it happen: our Senior Leadership Team allocated five staff hours per week to run the new council, agreed to out-of-school training, found office space for it, requested more regular meetings with teams, and found time at the beginning of the year to enable students to brief staff on the new model. The old school council attended summer sessions to make films for the student body about the changes, and three hours of PSHE lessons were set aside for the whole school to get up to speed with the new council.

I write in the run-up to the first elections of the new model school council. Its success will not be down to chance, afterthought or the ticking of a box. As with any school council, it will flourish or wither based on the capacity of students and teachers to work together in partnership, of teachers to listen to students' needs, of students to act independently on issues that they define. The council must be given the training, guidance and space to make changes to life and learning at the school. And the whole school – from the Headteacher down – must be involved.

Ben Hammond, Citizenship Co-ordinator, Deptford Green School

Other forms of consultation

In some schools, and on some issues, students' views are solicited directly (rather than through a council), through whole-school feasibility or evaluation studies or referenda on a specific issue. Student representatives are also sometimes included on decision-making panels – for staff appointments, during the tendering of contracts (for example for the school canteen), on the board of governors or committees that decide on punishments for frequent offenders.

School-level Citizenship initiatives

This approach is easiest to explain with an illustration. If, for example, the student council feels there should be more recycling around the school, young people themselves can be involved in considering different options for a recycling scheme and in ensuring that their chosen strategy runs smoothly. Not only will the students develop their Citizenship skills (researching, planning and executing a project), they are also more likely to use and promote the recycling facilities if they feel some ownership of the scheme. You will find another example in Figure 4.3, Chapter 4. As part of this unit of work taught to Year 8 at Bradford Academy, students wrote Fairtrade policies for the school, as well as creating posters and presentations promoting Fairtrade. The Principal of the Academy was involved in assessing the final pieces of work, and the school actually adopted the best Fairtrade policy, assessed by management and peers. In fact, at the instigation of the students, the school is now seeking to become the first school in Bradford to be recognized as a 'Fairtrade school' (a scheme run by the Fairtrade Foundation, and supported by the Department for International Development (DfID)). Figure 5.2 may be particularly useful during the planning of school-level projects like this. We have already touched on the six steps it outlines when discussing the importance of starting Citizenship teaching from issues relevant to students' lives (Chapter 3, 'Where to start?').

Peer support schemes

Peer involvement activities may include peer learning (academic), peer mentoring, counselling or conflict resolution (social). Such activities can provide opportunities for students to strengthen their ability to communicate their views, listen to and advocate the views of others, explore different approaches to a problem and assess the outcomes of their involvement. As ever, the more students are involved in planning and evaluation, the more they will develop their Citizenship skills.

Figure 5.2 Six steps for Citizenship projects

Step 1: Identifying the problem

You, or your students, may have already identified an issue for action; if not you could start by giving students time to explore, individually or in groups, what they think needs changing. What do they hate enough to make a difference to? What do they see that they think is unjust: at school, in their local communities, nationally or internationally? It is important that students feel a sense of ownership over their choice of issue, but it can also be practically helpful to limit their choice (for example to local or school issues). Help students to select one problem. What annoys them the most? Which of the problems do you and they think they could successfully make a change to?

Step 2: Researching the issue

The next step is finding out more about the issue. Students could use the internet, collect relevant newspaper articles, ask to see school policies or carry out interviews with other students, family or community members. What sources will be most helpful for their enquiry? What biases can they identify in these sources? What different viewpoints are there on the underlying problem? What has already been done to try and make a change? What do those affected think needs to be done? What do those who oppose change say? What do students think the crux of the problem is and what needs to be changed? Why?

Step 3: Selecting an action

What do students think they can do to make a difference? Encourage students to discuss their ideas, steering them to consider actions they have missed. Which actions do students think are relevant to their issue? What do they think the impact of their actions will be? What do their peers and families think? What about those affected? Which action do they think they can achieve, given the time and resources they have available?

Step 4: Planning the action

The next step is to draw up a plan of action. What do students need to do to complete their change action? What is their target date for completion? Can they assign different tasks to different members of the group? What resources do they have available to help them? Who could they ask for help? Can they complete the action in class-time, or will they need to organize some element of it out of class or school? If so, what do they need to know and consider in terms of risk assessment, insurance for out-of-school activities and transport?

Figure 5.2 (Continued)

Step 5: Carrying out the action

Students carry out their chosen action for change.

Step 6: Reflecting on the process

When students have completed their action for change, help them to reflect on how effective they were. To what extent did they achieve their aim? Were there any unintended impacts? Did they work well individually or as a team? What would they do differently next time to make their action more effective? Do they think the action they chose has any limitations? What more needs to be done to make the change they want? If they did not achieve their aim, why not?

Adapted from Brown (2008)

Citizenship beyond the school gates

Since Citizenship Education aims *'for people to think of themselves as active citizens, willing, able and equipped to have an influence in public life'* (QCA, 1998), it makes sense for that involvement in public life to start at school. This participation should not necessarily fall into a different category to the Citizenship taught in the classroom. We have already mentioned the importance of starting teaching from issues of relevance to young people's lives, which will often be issues beyond the school. Opportunities for students to talk or write to a prison warder, an environmental campaigner, a refugee or their MEP are often important elements of unit-planning. Lessons that include writing awareness-raising articles for a local newsletter, or action pledges to turn the TV off stand-by, can bring together participatory teaching and participation in the community. That community can be local, national or international: for example letters could be to a local councillor on the state of local leisure facilities, an MP on a national law or to a foreign government to request the release of political prisoners.

Opportunities for predetermined participation can be woven into most lessons, but the best, or at least most participatory, Citizenship projects are those where the ideas about what needs to be done come from the students. You have read, in earlier chapters, accounts of Citizenship projects that have brought about change in the local community and beyond. In the box opposite, dedicated Citizenship teacher Stuart George talks about facilitating student-led projects to teach in primary schools and clean up the local pond, among other actions. Such projects make an important contribution to his school's community cohesion agenda, exploring the school's links to the broader communities of which it is part. Figure 5.2 may be helpful when you plan or reflect on your, or your school's, community Citizenship projects.

Finally, it is worth noting that there are initiatives, at local and national levels, that already exist which some of your students may be interested in. For example, peer-elected members of the UK Youth Parliament (MYPs) meet regularly with other MYPs to discuss the issues they, and those they represent, want to see changed. They meet with local MPs and councillors, organize events, run campaigns, make speeches, hold debates and ensure their views are heard by decision makers.

In my 20s I came to the conclusion that people learn best when they are actively involved in things and that I had developed most as a person when ideas and projects I had put into practice had not gone according to plan! As a result I always told myself that any students I ended up teaching would be getting up off their backsides to get involved actively in the community.

Having now run many 'active citizenship' projects I am, if anything, a stronger advocate of such projects than ever before. What have these projects actually entailed? Here are some examples:

- Campaigning for a local cinema
- Planning and delivering a wide variety of lessons at primary schools
- An environment clean-up day at the local pond
- Putting together Christmas boxes for the elderly
- A fundraising and information day for the RSPCA, including a play
- Fundraising stalls and games for the NSPCC

These projects have been the fruition of Year 9 and 10 Citizenship lessons on the role of the Voluntary Sector. Overall the projects have engaged and united each class. I have, wherever possible, taken a back seat 'facilitator's' role. It has been proven to me time and time again that students have great ideas, passion and enthusiasm. In fact, one problem has sometimes been the need to rein that enthusiasm in! How often can that be said of a classroom-based lesson?

Inevitably problems and difficulties occur. Logistically it can be difficult. If off-site, do all students have parental permission? Extra staff may be needed to supervise the group. Transport may be required. There can be health and safety issues – Year 9 boys using saws at the

(Continued)

local pond springs to mind! Ultimately all such problems can be overcome. If you want to focus on these hassles and the extra work you have to undertake in facilitating these projects then maybe they will not work for you or your students. If, however, you focus on the learning and personal development that can take place, the enjoyment you can see your students experiencing, and the benefit and pleasure that community groups get from working constructively and collectively with young people, then it will work for you.

Following on from the projects, to acknowledge the work of our students and foster community links, our school recently held a 'celebration evening' to which students, family and friends, community partners and a dignitary or two were invited. The evening was a success and provided great PR for the school and for Citizenship within the school.

As alluded to earlier, things don't always go according to plan on such projects, and both I and the students continue to make errors along the way and wish that we had undertaken certain aspects differently. Now in my 30s I always remind myself of the learning there is to be had from making mistakes.

Stuart George, Head of Citizenship, Didcot Girls' School, Oxfordshire

Summary

We have a cartoon of a baseball-cap-and-trainer-clad youth, spray-painting a wall with the words 'Citisenship is Opresshun'. His teacher, seeing his handiwork, says to him *'You obviously feel very strongly about it, James, so why not expand it into a five-page essay and read it out in class?'* As citizens of today, rather than citizens in waiting, young people should be able to, indeed have a right to, express their views on issues that affect them. With their enormous capacity for outrage and sense of social justice, they are quick to spot injustice and identify the need for change. Our job as Citizenship teachers is to direct young people to the channels through which they are most able or likely to make a constructive difference, and support them to develop the skills they need to do so. Giving them opportunities for 'real' active citizenship, in the school and the community, is an important, not to mention statutory, way of doing this. We would want to engage the youth in the cartoon mentioned above in a discussion about the most effective ways of getting his message (which he has a right to communicate) across; which we might want to argue is neither through graffiti or through an essay.

Remember, finally, that participating in community projects and similar activities is not the end point of Citizenship Education. Students should be encouraged to reflect on the process of participation, and to think critically about why their participation was necessary. Raising money for Oxfam, for example, is not of itself Citizenship Education. It becomes Citizenship Education when young people reflect on the causes of poverty that make the work of organizations such as Oxfam important, and when they consider ways in which our societies address those problems, and how they can play a practical part.

Citizenship and cross-curricular initiatives   6

In recent years, a number of new curriculum initiatives have been introduced in English schools, for example: 'Every Child Matters'; 'community cohesion'; the 'global dimension'; and 'sustainable schools'. These new initiatives are all cross-curricular. There is a duty on all teachers, be they teachers of English, Mathematics, History, Geography or Science, to contribute to their provision in schools. Citizenship teachers are well positioned to take on some of that responsibility, and there are elements of the requirements where a clear connection can be made to Citizenship. Indeed there are some very specific requirements on Citizenship to address some of these issues. In this chapter we will explore those connections and endeavour to make clear what these initiatives might mean for you, as Citizenship teachers.

So what are these cross-curricular initiatives all about? They share a common background and philosophy, which is of itself interesting and worthy of comment at this stage. Problems of children's welfare, problems of fragmented communities and so called 'broken society', problems associated with globalization, such as the unfair distribution of resources and resultant poverty, and problems of environmental degradation and global warming are all problems of wider society. They are economic, political, social, legal and scientific problems. They are not, of themselves, surely, the problems of schools? Nonetheless, schools are invited by the legislation to contribute to the solution of society's problems by equipping young people with the knowledge and skills to engage with these issues and help to shape the future of the world they will inherit. These initiatives seem to move us towards providing an *education that develops in youth a competence in applying the best available strategies for survival in a world filled with unprecedented troubles, uncertainties and opportunities'* (Postman and Weingartner, 1969). Go back and look again at the list we cited from *Teaching as a Subversive Activity* in Chapter 1, and these initiatives look rather familiar; we told you that book was still relevant today!

A word of caution. Cross-curricular initiatives have always been problematic for secondary schools. There is an old aphorism that says 'something that is everybody's job, nobody does'. The History teacher may think *'I don't need to do that because the Geography teacher will do it, I'll just focus on the History syllabus.'* The Geography teacher decides to leave it to the English teacher, and guess what, the English teacher leaves it to the History teacher. There is a long history of failed or only partially successful cross-curricular initiatives in our schools. Remember, as we indicated in Chapter 1, that the first incarnation of National Curriculum Citizenship was as a cross-curricular theme, and only when the Crick report (QCA, 1998) recognized that the cross-curricular approach was not having the desired results (Potter, 2002) did the subject gain its own curriculum identity.

While it is beyond the scope of this book to address this question in detail, we digress for a moment to ask you to reflect on why the curriculum is divided up into 'subjects' at all? We would argue that 'subjects' are social constructs, they have no objective validity, but are merely convenient labels designed by human beings. Some have argued (you may have guessed that Postman and Weingartner are among them) that we should scrap 'subjects' as we currently know them in favour of a curriculum that encourages young people to ask questions, and seek the best answers to those questions wherever their enquiries may lead. Human knowledge does not need artificial boundaries: knowledge is knowledge. At what point in a discussion and enquiry in, for example, a History classroom does the teacher stop the class and say, *'That's not History, that's Geography'*, or *'Economics'*, or *'Science'* and bring the process of learning to an artificial close, and why?

If we are going to have subjects, which ones should we have? Why the particular labels that we have in our curriculum and why not others? *'Why history and geography? Why not cybernetics and ecology? Why economics and algebra? Why not anthropology and psycholinguistics? It is difficult to escape the feeling that a conventional curriculum is quite arbitrary in selecting the subjects to be studied'* (Postman and Weingartner, 1969). More food for your thoughts as you develop as a reflective practitioner.

Every Child Matters

In February 2000, an 8-year-old girl, Victoria Climbié, died after years of abuse by her legal guardians, who were later convicted of her murder. An inquiry into the child's death, led by Lord Laming, found that various agencies involved in Victoria's care, her schools, her social workers and the health service, had each recorded concerns about aspects of her welfare and yet had failed to intervene. However, information in the hands of each of the individual agencies was not shared with the other agencies. Had it been shared, patterns might have been recognized that may have led to such an intervention. *The Victoria Climbié Inquiry*, also known as the Laming report (2003), recommended that in future all of the agencies involved in child welfare issues should share the information they have access to with the others.

In 2003 the government launched the Every Child Matters (ECM) initiative. This is a multi-agency initiative designed to achieve five key outcomes that are held to be essential to children's wellbeing: health; safety; enjoyment and achievement; making a contribution; and economic wellbeing. The government's intention that there should be information sharing *'between schools and other agencies about individual children with additional needs . . . supported by new databases or indexes containing basic information about each child or young person that will enable schools to make contact more easily with other practitioners'* (DfES, 2004) is clearly influenced by the Laming report. ECM was followed in 2004 by the Children Act, and also explains why, in 2008, the previous Department for Education and Skills evolved into the Department for Children, Schools and Families, to continue the process of unifying children's services.

The Climbié case (and the more recent case of Baby P, details of which were emerging as this book was going to print) is of course horrific, an extreme example of the maltreatment of a child. Fortunately such extreme cases are rare, but there has also been a growing concern in recent years about lesser instances of abuse of children, not only by adults, but by their peers. Concerns about bullying, often for no apparent reason, but sometimes because of intolerance of others to differences in ethnicity, religious beliefs or sexuality, have also informed ECM. Campaigns such as those organized by 'Childline' have been influential in developing the agenda, and the current concerns about knife crime on our cities' streets, where young people are both the perpetrators and victims of crime, are also relevant.

In schools, ECM is both a curriculum and pastoral initiative. ECM is intended to raise educational standards by *'encouraging schools to offer a range of extended services that help pupils engage and achieve, and building stronger relationships with parents and the wider community; and supporting closer working between universal services so that children with additional needs can be identified earlier and supported effectively'* (DfES, 2004).

A key part of ECM is 'student voice'; the principle that children and young people have the right to be heard and listened to. Young people, better than any of us, know the problems they face, and they have a right to be involved in suggesting and developing the solutions. Citizenship, with its emphasis on developing the skills of expressing a point of view, individually and collectively, and of campaigning for change and participating in decision making, is uniquely placed to assist in the development of student voice.

ECM's intended outcomes include giving students opportunities to: 'engage in decision making and support the community and environment'; 'engage in law-abiding and positive behaviour in and out of school'; and 'develop positive relationships and choose not to bully and discriminate' (DfES, 2004). Clear connections may be seen between each of these intended outcomes and elements of the process and content of Citizenship Education, where students gain experience of 'participating actively in different kinds of decision making and voting in order to influence public life'; explore 'the role of law in maintaining order and resolving conflict'; and 'develop respect for the views and rights of others, and the importance of tolerance' (QCA, 2007). Accordingly, it is clear that Citizenship teachers have a major curriculum contribution to make towards ECM.

As a Citizenship teacher I had to think about which aspects of ECM I could make a direct contribution to. I felt there were many, but here are some examples.

Be healthy

While this clearly has a link to PSHEE, there is also a focus for Citizenship if we take a wider viewpoint, in particular if we consider *access* to health.

Students could consider the case of Jane Tomlinson and the problems of postcode lotteries regarding treatment for cancer and other conditions (this story is available in newspapers from October 2007). After considering the issues around this, students could engage in a debate, one side representing the health authority defending their decision, another representing a patient advocacy group arguing for equality of access to medication.

Alternatively students can debate whether health should be free for all, or whether people who precipitate ill health, by smoking or eating poorly, should have to pay for conditions linked to smoking/high fat food.

Stay safe

This area can be concerned about law and order, and how to stay safe. Students could focus on personal safety, and have a visit from a local

(Continued)

police officer who can discuss crime prevention for young people. In addition, older students could perhaps visit a local primary school to allay fears about bullying, and talk about safety on the journey to school. Alternatively, older students could consider issues like drink spiking and drug use – local drugs support agencies may provide visitors to work with students.

Enjoy and achieve

This area really lends itself to the study of rights and responsibilities. Students can look at how their own school helps them achieve their best, and recommend changes through the student council as to how they can be improved. Students can look at education in Africa and China, and compare experiences. In particular, students could engage in activities such as 'Send my friend to school' (www.sendmyfriend.org).

Make a positive contribution

Of the five outcomes, this is perhaps the most obviously linked to Citizenship. Students could engage in projects in school or in the local community that 'add value' in some way. For example, creating a sensory garden for a local school for children with special needs, or engaging in 'community clean-ups', perhaps linking up with other local environmental organizations and learning more about the local environment.

Achieve economic wellbeing

Financial capability is becoming increasingly important as more people find themselves in debt. Many high street banks offer financial capability teaching resources such as Natwest's 'Holiday Planner' where students attempt to budget for a dream holiday to Florida. By linking this to enterprise skills, students could set up a mini-business, either by creating memorabilia to sell for a school play, or creating team flags for a sports day. They then play a game like 'Trading Trainers' and consider the differences in wages and conditions between their business and those in the developing world. If coming up to a general election, students could look at the financial pledges made by each political party, and consider which party would be the most economically suitable for their own family.

Linda Asquith, formerly Head of Citizenship and PSHE,
Wakefield Cathedral High School

Citizenship Education, and ECM, are not just about what happens in schools and the classroom. There is no point in us helping young people to develop Citizenship skills if they are not, in a very real sense, to be used. We have cited the Crick report's point that 'we aim at no less than a change in the political culture of this country' (QCA, 1998). Children and young people are no longer to be 'seen and not heard'. As we have indicated, ECM is a multi-agency initiative, so it is not sufficient that student voice be heard just in and by schools and teachers, but also by other professionals and agencies involved in decision making about their lives and welfare. ECM (partially informed by the UN Convention on the Rights of the Child) is about the democratization of children's and young people's services, and involves guidance to schools and other agencies, (and to young people themselves), about how this might happen in practice (Kirby et al., 2003).

Community cohesion

In April 1993, an 18-year-old boy called Stephen Lawrence was murdered on a street in south London because of the colour of his skin. In July 2008, an 18-year-old boy called Michael Causer was murdered on a street in Liverpool because of his sexuality. Between May and July 2001, there were three incidences of rioting by groups of British Asian youth, on the streets of Oldham (May), Burnley (June) and Bradford (July), involving cars and properties being firebombed, and missiles thrown at the police. A few days after the initial riots in Bradford, up to 100 white youths staged a 'counter-attack', a second riot, firebombing an Asian-owned restaurant in the process. Twenty years earlier British West Indians had rioted on the streets of Brixton and Toxteth. On 7 July 2005, a young man who had been born and raised in West Yorkshire led a group of other young men in a terrorist attack on London, these young men taking their own lives in the process. There is a current 'moral panic' about the extent of gun and knife crime among young people in our cities, and an apparent rise in gang culture. For the last 30 years there has been a steadily widening gap between rich and poor in our society. There is a 'north–south' divide, and in August 2008, a right-wing 'think tank', Policy Exchange, argued that the economic problems of cities such as Bradford, Liverpool and Sunderland were such that they were beyond solution. Our media, and numerous politicians, have spoken of a broken society, fragmented into small parts with little communication between them.

Various reports have been commissioned into some of these divisions. The *Scarman Report* into the Brixton riots (1981) pointed to the deep economic and social problems of the area, and the deep mistrust of the police by black youngsters because of the perceived racism inherent in police 'stop and search tactics'. The *Stephen Lawrence Inquiry* (Macpherson, 1999) investigated Stephen Lawrence's death and made a total of 70 recommendations for reform (and also commented on the failure of the Metropolitan Police to act to address shortcomings in their policies and practice identified by Scarman). The Macpherson proposals included a call for reform in the police, the civil service, the NHS, schools and the judicial system, in order to address issues of institutional racism. The Ouseley report, into social fragmentation in Bradford (*Community Pride, Not Prejudice. Making Diversity Work in Bradford*, 2001), pointed to segregation between communities in the city, which extended even to the schools; some schools containing predominantly white children, while others contained predominantly British Asians. The report stressed the need to strengthen partnerships between community groups, for better education about diversity issues, and for deep changes in attitudes and behaviour across communities. The Cantle report, into the Oldham riots (*Challenging Local Communities to Change Oldham*, 2006), pointed to similar divisions and polarization between different ethnic communities, and a reluctance of sections of the community, including community leaders, to embrace positive change.

To digress from the main theme of this chapter for a moment; each and every one of these issues is controversial, as is each and every one of these reports. Each would be rich and legitimate territory for investigation, discussion and debate in a Citizenship classroom in and of themselves (for example, see the work done by Aashiya Chaus in Challenge College, Bradford, pp. 111–12).

It is against this background that schools have been required to include in their curriculum a community cohesion agenda. Community cohesion means '*working towards a society in which there is a common vision and sense of belonging by all communities; a society in which the diversity of people's backgrounds and circumstances is appreciated and valued; a society in which similar opportunities are available to all; and a society in which strong and positive relationships exist and continue to be developed in the workplace, in schools and in the wider community*' (DCSF, 2007). A MORI survey for DCSF found considerable evidence of barriers to community cohesion, '*mistrust of different groups, particularly those new to the local community, a perception that local authorities are giving others special treatment*', a lack of community spirit and a lack of facilities where those of different social backgrounds might interact. '*Cohesion is therefore about how to avoid the corrosive effects of intolerance and harassment: how to build a mutual civility among different groups, and to ensure respect for diversity alongside a commitment to common and shared bonds'* (DCSF, 2007).

Schools were identified as having a key role to play in promoting community cohesion in a number of ways. First, schools need to provide genuine equality of opportunity for all young people, regardless of class, ethnicity, gender or sexuality. Schools need to be places that exemplify tolerance and mutual respect; with teachers having a key role to play both in modelling these qualities and ensuring that their students show these courtesies to each other. Community cohesion is not just about ethnic and religious tensions. *'Race and faith are often seen as the most frequent friction points between communities, and the most visible sources of tension. However, discrimination and prejudice can be experienced by other groups – including the disabled, Lesbian, Gay, Bisexual and Transgender communities and different age and gender groups'* (DCSF, 2007). Schools need to tackle the full range of bullying and discriminatory behaviour, and language. It should be just as unacceptable for children to be using the word 'gay' in a derogatory manner (as seems currently fashionable) as it is to use terms of racist abuse.

Schools are not (or should not be) isolated institutions; they are communities in and of themselves but are also part of wider communities, local, national and global. The community cohesion agenda encourages schools to explore and develop their links to the broader communities of which they are part. Immediately we hope that you can see, in this agenda, multiple connections to the Citizenship curriculum; connections that have been present ever since the first draft of National Curriculum Citizenship, implemented in schools from September 2002. However, just in case, in the new version of the Citizenship curriculum, for implementation from September 2008, the connection is made much more explicit

In January 2007, Sir Keith Ajegbo (recently retired as Headteacher of Deptford Green school in south London, a multi-ethnic school with a strong reputation for Citizenship Education), produced a report that had been commissioned by the Secretary of State for Education. The Ajegbo report (*Diversity and Citizenship Curriculum Review*, 2007) recommended that a fourth 'strand' (to supplement the Crick report's suggested strands of social and moral responsibility, community involvement and political literacy) be introduced to the Citizenship curriculum; *Identities and Diversity: Living Together in the UK* (QCA, 2007). Ajegbo argued that schools needed to address in the curriculum a range of controversial issues around who we are, how we live together and how we deal with our differences. Interestingly, Ajegbo was at pains to point out how working-class white males had become a marginalized, neglected and resultantly disengaged and resentful group, as a result of perceptions that schools and policy makers were addressing agendas that celebrated and recognized the identity of others but not their own. Such youth, argued Ajegbo, had lost their sense of identity, and wondered what it was to be 'British'.

The 2007 rewrite of the Citizenship National Curriculum took on board Ajegbo's recommendations, and explicitly requires the exploration of *'community cohesion and the different forces that bring about change in communities over time'* (QCA, 2007). Study of Citizenship should include the origins of the diverse communities that make up the UK, their shared heritage (for example in Europe or the Commonwealth) as well as understanding of, and respect for, their differences. This study needs to include the history of all the varied peoples of the British Isles, of whatever ethnicity, and their roles in shaping our society and our world.

The global dimension

From September 2008, schools have a duty to incorporate teaching about the global dimension across the curriculum. Concern about the global dimension is not new. For nearly 40 years an informal national network of local development education centres, such as Leeds Development Education Centre (Leeds DEC), Birmingham's Teachers in Development Education (TIDE), Reading International Solidarity Centre (RISC) and Norfolk Education and Action for Development (NEAD) have been enthusiastic advocates for Development Education (DE). In 1991 the Development Education Association was formed as an umbrella group for these and other DE organizations (Cameron and Fairbrass, 2004). In 2005 DEA and DfID published *Developing the Global Dimension in the School Curriculum*. More recently, DfID funded nine regional initiatives, such as the East Anglian Development Education Network (EADEN) and the Yorkshire and Humberside Global Schools Association (YHGSA), to promote and coordinate teaching about the global dimension in schools. Campaigning by the DE movement, with support from DfID, has eventually led to the September 2008 development.

Development Education has a radical history. The principles of DE are about methodology and pedagogy, every bit as much as about content. Informed by the writings of Paolo Freire (1970), who himself drew on the work of Antonio Gramsci (see Hoare and Nowell-Smith, 1971), DE adopted an active, participative, student-centred approach to learning; and most importantly development educators saw their role as empowering learners to take action for change. It is not difficult, therefore, to see close parallels between DE and Citizenship Education, and indeed some of the best Citizenship Education initiatives have borrowed heavily from a DE methodology.

Besides a shared pedagogical approach, a clear link in conceptual and subject knowledge content exists between 'the global dimension' and Citizenship Education. The Citizenship curriculum requires the study of Citizenship to include *'the UK's relations with the European Union and the rest of Europe, the Commonwealth, the United Nations and the world as a global community'* (QCA, 2007). Students in Citizenship should *'consider the interconnections between the UK and the rest of Europe and the wider world'*, *'analyse the impact of their actions on communities and the wider world, now and in the future'* and *'take into account a range of contexts such as . . . international and global as relevant to different topics'* (ibid). Accordingly, besides the general requirement on all subjects to include a global dimension, there is a clear and explicit requirement for this dimension to be explored in Citizenship Education programmes.

Perhaps we should declare an interest; we both came into Citizenship Education from backgrounds in Development Studies and Development Education. We are accordingly acutely aware of the connections, and the particular strengths and depths which a truly global dimension can add to Citizenship Education programmes.

Figure 6.1 School linking

School linking, or relationships between two or more schools, has become a very popular, and indeed government supported, phenomena. In particular, school links have been encouraged in response to the community cohesion and global dimension agendas. Advocates claim that relationships between schools in different parts of the same city, or in rural and urban parts of the same county, allow young people from different ethnic groups and backgrounds to learn from each other. Relationships between schools in the UK and schools in the 'global south', if well thought out, may enable students to gain a greater global perspective.

In both cases, a link is a 'real' window on another place, and linking activities (such as joint curriculum projects or even physical exchanges) can be engaging and motivating. However, to be successful, links must be supported at a senior level, embedded in the curriculum, and developed with input from both partner schools. In this respect, 'overseas' links have been particularly controversial, with some people questioning whether linking achieves the learning outcomes attributed to it (Brown, 2006), and others concerned about the power

(Continued)

relationships between partner schools (for example, see Leonard, 2008). Certainly, these are issues to be considered if you are involved in establishing or developing a link between your school and another. There are lots of organizations that can offer you information, advice and support (see Chapter 8). Below, we briefly mention what we think are four priorities for school linking.

Embed the school link in the curriculum

Links need to go beyond the exchange of occasional letters. The catch-phrase is that the school link should be sustained and 'embedded in the curriculum': students should be exposed to the link throughout their whole school experience. That might be through subject-specific projects based on the exchange of information, collapsed timetable events or learning about the locality of the partner school in different subjects (for example, the geography, history or poetry of the area).

Be creative

The Schools Linking Network, which supports links between UK schools (read more about their work in Chapter 8), has found that creativity is fundamental to developing the space for dialogue between students. Being imaginative about the projects your schools develop together ensures that the work really is engaging and motivating.

Listen to your link school

For the link to be a true partnership, both partners must have equal input into the direction the link takes. This is particularly an issue if your link is with a school in the 'global south': unequal access to resources and technology can mean that the school in the 'north' has more control. Some question whether a truly equal partnership is ever possible in these circumstances. Whether or not this is the case, a good start is a commitment to understanding the needs and ideas of your partner school, so that you can develop the agenda of your link together.

Think about the role of fundraising

Again, this is generally more an issue with 'overseas' linking, when a large element of the partnership may revolve around fundraising. While this can certainly provide an opportunity for students to see the impact of their actions, there is a concern that it can also reinforce a sense of a poor, helpless 'other'. On the other hand, students may be motivated to initiate fundraising, the partner school is likely to have material needs and one of their aims in linking may be to access funds, which cannot be ignored. However, fundraising needs to be carefully considered and handled, and the relationship should be about more than just raising money.

Sustainable schools

In May 2006, DfES issued a consultation paper about developing sustainable schools, which began by inviting schools and others to contribute to a debate about sustainability. *'DfES has reaffirmed its commitment to sustainable development by publishing a two-year action plan to achieve outcomes to underpin a sustainable society. Schools are a key strand of this action plan and are invited to become models of sustainable development for their communities. This consultation paper seeks views from schools and their stakeholders on how we can work together to turn issues like climate change, global justice and local quality of life into engaging learning opportunities for pupils – and a focus for action among the whole school community'* (DfES, 2006). The consultation led to the establishment of a national framework, backed by a website, for the development of sustainable schools.

The national framework identifies eight gateways through which a sustainable development agenda might be embedded into whole-school management approaches. These are: food and drink; energy and water; travel and traffic; purchasing and waste; buildings and grounds; inclusion and participation; local wellbeing; and the global dimension.

If you have followed our story so far about the Citizenship curriculum requirements, and the other cross-curricular initiatives, we hope we don't have to spend too much time in pointing out the connections here. For example, the links between sustainability and globalization are well-developed territory and local wellbeing links to the ECM wellbeing agenda. Energy generation and use, and energy conservation (and the links to transport and congestion), are all examples of controversial issues that might be discussed in a Citizenship classroom. Citizenship requires that young people have opportunities to engage in real decision making about issues that affect them and their communities, and where better to begin than within the school community where they spend so much of their lives. Citizenship encourages the democratization of decision making in schools, and we are aware of schools that have consulted their students on many of these issues, for example: purchasing of recycled paper exercise books; school recycling policies; provision of fairly traded, organically produced and/or GM-free food and drinks in student catering facilities; safe and clean play areas and facilities. We have discussed in Chapter 5 the importance, and relevance to Citizenship, of opportunities for students to participate in the life of the school.

A cautionary note: the challenge to Citizenship Education

As we have previously mentioned, when Citizenship was first introduced to the curriculum it was as a cross-curricular initiative. Since September 2002, Citizenship has been a National Curriculum foundation subject at Key Stage 3 and Key Stage 4, a subject with equal status in the curriculum to History, Geography, etc. However, many schools have failed to fully recognize this legal change in status, or the difference in standing between statutory Citizenship and non-statutory PSHEE.

There is a risk that in some schools the new agendas of ECM, community cohesion, the global dimension and sustainable schools will simply be loaded on to an already overcrowded PSHEE and Citizenship curriculum space, while other subjects get on with the 'important' business of preparing students for the examinations that will determine the school's standing in league tables. Hopefully, the fact that the new agendas are subject to inspection by Ofsted will go some way to alleviating this risk, but it is not something about which we can afford to be complacent.

In this context, we caution and urge Citizenship specialists not to allow their subject to be overwhelmed by the new initiatives and lose its unique identity and space in the timetable. Citizenship must defend its status and territory just as History and Science will. Citizenship teachers have a major contribution to make to ECM, community cohesion, the global dimension and sustainable schools; but it is everybody's responsibility, not just ours. Our curriculum time and space is limited, and there are many other things we also need to do.

Summary

There is a clear synergy between key elements of the Citizenship curriculum and these cross-curricular initiatives. Indeed there are synergies between the various initiatives. A DCSF spokesperson was quoted as saying *'Learning about the global dimension can also provide schools with opportunities to promote community cohesion and, in partnership with families, develop skills that will enable young people to combat injustice, prejudice and discrimination. It provides young people with opportunities to critically examine their own values and attitudes and appreciate and contrast them with other cultures'* (Tickle, 2008).

We hope that, like us, you can see links between ECM and community cohesion: both emphasizing respect for others, tolerance of difference and awareness of shared values; both emphasizing the need to communicate, within the school and within wider communities; and both hoping to promote community safety and individual wellbeing, free of bullying and violence. In both the ECM and community cohesion agenda, and inherently in Citizenship, the notion of 'student voice', of young people engaging with, and helping to determine policy in their communities, within and beyond school, is paramount.

Globalization and sustainability are inextricably linked themes, and of concern to academics in a range of fields: politicians, economists, sociologists and scientists all have something to say on these issues. 'Think global, act local' has become the mantra of many environmental, Development Education and campaigning groups and is implicit in the Citizenship curriculum. *'Every one of our actions, as citizens, consumers and producers, has both local and global consequences. In global citizenship terms there is no other, there is just we'* (Fairbrass, 2004).

All of these issues are current, controversial and open to debate. All of these issues are of concern to us as citizens of the UK, Europe and the world, and all of them merit debate in the Citizenship classroom.

Assessment in Citizenship   **7**

Assessment is a vital part of the educational process. Well-designed assessment is not an adjunct to, but an integral part of, the day-to-day business of teaching and learning. However, assessment is a problematic area in education generally, and in Citizenship Education specifically. Ofsted (2003) reported that *'assessment is currently a weak aspect of Citizenship'*. As teachers of Citizenship we need to consider why we assess, what we assess and how we assess. These are more complex questions than they may at first appear. Assessment is not just a technical issue, but also a highly political one, and therefore controversial (indeed, educational assessment policies might themselves make an interesting topic for investigation and discussion in a Citizenship classroom). Judgements are made about schools based on the results of their students in SATs, GCSE and GCE examinations, and league tables drawn up. Governments boast of 'good' examination results, or are castigated by their opponents for 'poor' ones. Demagogues in the media periodically tell us that 'standards are slipping', things are 'not what they were' and so on. In the midst of all this, teachers have to get on with the day-to-day task of assessment.

We begin this chapter with a brief consideration of some of the principles by which students work and progress might be assessed, and, through these, illustrate just some of the past and present controversies around assessment; there are many more. We then go on to consider 'assessment for learning'; the contribution assessment makes to the everyday business of education, and some thoughts about practical approaches to assessment in Citizenship, including some case study examples. From there we go on to consider 'assessment of learning'; the formal requirements on us as teachers to carry out assessments for the purpose of reporting to parents and others, and the examinations system. We encourage you throughout to recognize and engage in the problematic nature of the terrain of assessment. We recommend that you read around the topic of assessment very thoroughly: good places to start are Black and William (1998) and Black *et al.* (2002), which you will find listed in the bibliography.

Principles of assessment

There are essentially three principles or standards that we might use to benchmark assessments; norm referenced, criterion referenced and ipsative assessments.

In norm referenced assessment we may have in mind some notion of an average expectation of learning and achievement, for the class or year group as a whole. We might then consider any individual student's progress relative to that norm. Is the student better, equal to or worse than the average or norm? We may carry out some assessment or test, for example, and award 'top' grades to a certain predetermined percentage of the group (the best 30% perhaps). We award 'middle' grades to the next group (say the next 40%) and 'bottom' (or 'fail') grades to the last group (the remaining 30%) because our expectation is that we have 30% 'good' students, 40% 'average' students and 30% 'weak' students.

Alternatively, assessment may be criterion referenced; we may have some set or list of external criteria against which we assess an individual, and make judgements about which of those criteria have been met. If all of the criteria are met, then a 'top' grade is awarded, moving down to lower grades as there are differing levels of partial achievement of the criteria. Finally we may have 'fail' grades for those who do not succeed in meeting any of the criteria.

The debate about norm or criterion referenced assessment is a real one, though you may not have seen it expressed in those terms. Each year, in August, the results of GCSE and GCE examinations are published. Each year the achievements of the young people who have passed those examinations are routinely denigrated by the popular press. Record numbers of people have passed, therefore the examinations must be getting easier, the headlines proclaim. Implicitly, the press are adopting a norm referenced view of assessment. They are assuming that there is some kind of normal distribution of 'ability' that only a certain percentage of the population possess. But the modern GCSE and GCE examination system is a criteria based system. A set of criteria are established for each grade, and any individual who meets those criteria is awarded the grade. The fact that more people are achieving those criteria is not necessarily an indication that 'standards are slipping', rather an indication that teaching (and learning) are improving, at least in terms of achieving whatever these examinations measure. While we would happily join in a discussion about whether our examination system has any real educational relevance, would be willing to contribute to a critique of the system and have views on how it could be improved (starting with scrapping the whole thing and beginning over again), we challenge the rather simplistic notion that examinations are simply 'getting easier'. That really is missing the point.

Consider this sporting analogy. In 1954 Roger Bannister became the first man (or at least, the first recorded) to run a mile in under four minutes. Before the 50th anniversary of Bannister's achievement 955 more men had replicated the feat, several more than once, between them achieving it some 4700 times (*New York Times*, 4 May 2003). Has the mile become shorter, or has running it become easier? The truth is that better coaching, better understanding of training needs, improvements in athletes' fitness, improved nutrition regimes and many other factors have contributed to more people being able to achieve the criterion.

One of the classic norm referenced assessments was the now (thankfully) largely defunct '11+' examination. The 1944 Education Act, which established the 'tripartite system' of grammar schools, technical schools and secondary modern schools, made an assumption that a certain fixed proportion of children had the academic ability each year to benefit from a grammar school education. The 11+ would identify those children, the most able x%, who would be awarded the places. This is a norm referenced system.

The 11+ system fell into disrepute (and was wound up from the late 1960s onwards, except in a few diehard LEAs) for a variety of reasons, not least because it was recognized that it operated more as a lottery than a real form of assessment. For example, each local authority had to decide for itself how many grammar school (and how many technical and secondary modern) places to provide. The opportunity to go to a grammar school was determined purely by the number of places available. If 250 places were available each year in an area, then 250 students each year would 'pass' the 11+. A mark that in the examination one year might be sufficient to secure a grammar school place might not be sufficient the following year, if more people exceeded it. A mark achieved in one town/county, which provided grammar school places for 10% of its children, might not be sufficient to achieve a place, whereas it might do so in a neighbouring area where 35% of children were provided with places. There was also disparity (in an era when single sex schools were more prevalent) between the number of grammar school places available to girls and boys.

The PGCE courses which most of you are taking, or have taken, and which lead to the award of Qualified Teacher Status (QTS) are essentially assessed on a criterion referenced basis. The Training and Development Agency for Schools (TDA) set a kind of 'national curriculum' for teacher training; the QTS standards. To be recommended for the award of QTS, trainee teachers must demonstrate that they have satisfied each of 33 'standards' or criteria. Satisfy the criteria and you earn the award – there is no quota or limit to the number of people allowed to pass (although there are quotas laid down by TDA for the number of people allowed on to the courses in the first place).

Increasingly, there is a growth of interest in ipsative assessment regimes; we assess progress of an individual against that person's own previous performance, and note that the individual has improved (they can do something now that they could not do previously), remained the same or worsened. For example, imagine a 'fun runner' who decides to take part in the London Marathon. After a year of training, she completes the run in six hours, a time that has not threatened the leaders; Paula Radcliffe's world record is safe for now. A year later the same runner has another go at the event. This time she completes the 26 miles 385 yards in 5 hours 35 minutes. Again, the time is way off the pace of the winner, but a real improvement, and a real achievement for this individual. Note that in ipsative assessment there is no concept of failure. Ipsative assessment is closely associated with ideas about the personalizing and individualization of learning; issues that we have mentioned in Chapter 6 in association with the Every Child Matters agenda.

Each of these approaches to assessment has its advantages, and each has its shortcomings. We hope that you have already begun to be concerned, and perhaps have reservations, about aspects of each of the above principles of assessment, and are already thinking critically about them. In the UK, over the last few decades, we have seen a general (but by no means universal) tendency towards norm based assessment regimes being replaced by criterion based systems, and there is some evidence (albeit not without some considerable resistance) of movement in the direction of ipsative forms of assessment.

We invite you to further explore this territory. You will need to make decisions on the assessment regimes you introduce, and why and how you report assessment results back to your students and others. We leave you with the thought that assessment itself is a 'controversial issue', and the arguments about it are political as well as educational.

Assessment for learning in Citizenship

As we teach, as our students learn, we need to continually monitor the students', and our own, progress. We need to be sure that learning is taking place, and we need to understand what is actually being learned. Constant assessment (and reflection) of this kind informs our teaching, and students' learning. By understanding, on a day-to-day basis, what our students have learned, we can make judgements on the success of our own teaching. This enables us to modify what we do if we feel that our learning objectives (or learning targets students set for themselves) are not being achieved. We can identify individuals who are making more progress or less progress than we hope or expect (relative to some norm, or some criterion or to their own previous progress), and tailor our teaching and the development of learning experiences to their individual needs.

Assessment for learning, formative assessment, is continual, and gives us the opportunity to offer feedback to learners about their progress, which in turn enables them to make further progress. As we have indicated in Chapter 3, it is essential that the process of assessment in Citizenship is embedded in the pedagogical process. Opportunities for assessment should be identified, and planned for, at the stage of designing schemes of work and lesson plans, *'planned from the beginning as part of teaching and learning'* (QCA, 2006). As part of the process of setting learning objectives, and hoped for learning outcomes, we should include the identification of strategies for assessing whether the objectives and outcomes have been achieved. Some assessment may be formal and recorded (perhaps some kind of learning log of progress towards a target over time), some assessment may be informal (perhaps a five-minute 'question and answer' session at the end of a lesson). Questioning also gives students an opportunity to reflect on their own learning: both when they answer questions, and when they hear others' answers and are able to compare their own levels of understanding. All assessments are important.

QCA (2006) suggest: *'Improving learning through assessment depends on five key principles: providing effective feedback to pupils, actively involving pupils in their own learning, adjusting teaching to take account of the results of assessment, recognising the profound influence assessment has on the motivation and self-esteem of pupils, both of which are crucial influences on learning, pupils being able to assess themselves and understand how to improve.'* We will endeavour to suggest ways that this might be achieved, and give examples of how it is being done in some schools.

Practical strategies for assessment for learning in Citizenship

The National Curriculum for Citizenship gives us a start point for the planning of assessment. As we have indicated in Chapter 2, the Citizenship curriculum requires students to develop an understanding of concepts such as human rights, to develop key skills such as the ability to express and explain their opinions, to acquire a range of knowledge such as understanding the way in which the justice system operates and to have opportunities to engage in practical, citizenship activities such as decision making and campaigning. So assessment should, at the very least, focus on whether these requirements are being met: whether students are indeed able to do those things that the curriculum requires that they be able to do. It is also important that assessment in Citizenship should be inclusive, that it gives all students, whatever their aptitudes and abilities, a chance to record and have their work validated; a celebration of what has been achieved. Assessment needs to *'reflect the learning and achievements of all pupils and take account of their learning styles and intelligences'* (QCA, 2006). We need to plan for the assessment of work in a multitude of forms, including written work, oral work, visual work and practical work. We need also to consider who will actually be involved in the assessment process. Teachers clearly have a key role to play in assessment. However, central to the pedagogy of Citizenship Education (as we have suggested in Chapter 3) is a commitment to participative and experiential learning opportunities, learning by doing, democracy in action. It would be perverse if the assessment of Citizenship did not also adopt these approaches, so students themselves need to be active participants in the assessment process, both as self and peer assessors. Indeed the Key Stage 4 Citizenship curriculum requires that students *'reflect on the progress they have made, evaluating what they have learnt from the intended and unintended consequences of action, and the contributions of others as well as themselves'* (QCA, 2007).

Self and peer assessment are a key focus of teacher training, and really important when in school. Getting students actively involved in the learning process, and evaluating their progress and that of others, is vital. It can also help lighten the marking load for a burdened teacher if organized effectively! My initial suspicions were that students would not take it seriously and just give each other top marks without thought – but I have been surprised by how they respond to the responsibility and often mark each other's work with more care and attention than I would! For some teachers peer and self-assessment

(Continued)

come naturally and they involve it in many lessons. For me it was more of a conscious effort and I had to think quite carefully about how I would include it.

One approach I found worked well involved peer teaching as well as peer assessing. During my time teaching I have found that students learn best when they are teaching each other. They take in the information better this way. I identify a topic in which this can work well first. To introduce it, we spend a while discussing what makes a good and bad teacher. We also discuss how a lesson should be laid out, and lessons they have enjoyed. They then get into groups, research the topic and prepare a lesson. I will help them with this, questioning their ideas and checking that their lesson will be engaging and that there will be ways they can measure student progress. They then get the opportunity to deliver their lesson to the class and receive constructive feedback along the 'what went well' and 'even better if' lines. I have found this method of peer assessment fosters teamwork, presenting skills and confidence. I have often been impressed with their ideas and been forced to declare 'I'm done for, my job is yours!'

Emily Miller, Citizenship teacher with TeachFirst,
North Manchester High School for Girls

However, once we have opened the possibility of people other than teachers having a role to play in assessment, should we just stop at the students? Are there others in the school and/or beyond its gates who might legitimately be involved in the process? In a workshop on Assessment in Citizenship Education given in 2003, Lee Jerome argued that other stakeholders might have valid contributions to make. For example, if students from a school were involved in some kind of Citizenship community project outside of school, then the views of the beneficiaries of that project, or community partners who worked with the students, might be sought in the assessment process.

We next need to consider what kinds of data (which might be quantitative or qualitative) will provide us with evidence of development, progress and achievement. We also need to consider how that data will be collected, what the success criteria will be, and where and how the results of assessment will be recorded. Once again, in the best Citizenship classrooms, involving real learning for democracy, the students themselves have a role to play in making these decisions.

A tool such as the one below might be useful in planning assessment through a module or unit of work, or over a period of time, and for guiding the thoughts of both the teacher and the students (and other stakeholders as appropriate).

Figure 7.1 Planning assessment through a unit of work

What are we assessing?	Who will carry out the assessment?	What kinds of data will provide evidence of achievement?	How will the data be collected?	What are the success criteria?	Where and how will the evidence be recorded?
Citizenship concepts					
Citizenship skills					
Citizenship knowledge					
Citizenship participation					

Citizenship subject knowledge, and to some extent understanding of Citizenship concepts, might be most easily assessed through quizzes, tests and examinations. These can be administered orally, or in writing, and can be very formal or quite informal. How many Members of Parliament are there? Explain the 'first past the post' electoral system by which they get elected. How does Parliament create laws? What is the difference between civil and criminal law, between judges and magistrates? Explain the process, and the advantages, of trial by jury. What does the EU do? What are human rights? How does the existence of a free press help to ensure our rights? Through questions such as these we can assess factual knowledge, and some degree of understanding. We can begin to assess higher order skills such as the ability to analyse, evaluate and synthesize, for example *'weighing up what is fair and unfair in different situations'* (QCA, 2007), depending on the precise questions we pose and the space/ time we allow students to answer.

It is important, however, that we recognize that some young people find testing processes, examinations and the like, intimidating, and are not able to give their best in those situations (McIntyre, 1972). There is also considerable research evidence from a number of studies that low achieving students are demoralized by the award of low marks, and that these deter them from further effort; hardly what we want to see if our purpose in assessment is to guide students on how they might improve. It is worth thinking creatively about this. An activity like 'Citizenship Bingo' turns assessment into a game. A series of questions are posed on a handout. However, rather than answering the questions themselves, students have the task of finding others who can answer the questions for them; a different person for each question. The first person to gather answers to each question, from as many people as there are questions, 'wins' the bingo game. Assessment can, and we believe should, be presented to young people as part of the process of learning, and an aid to their progress, rather than a series of hurdles that must be jumped over (and with the possibility of falling). If assessment (as well as learning) is fun and enjoyable, and not judgemental, the intimidation can be removed.

Testing and the like are not, however, particularly or at all, appropriate strategies for assessing the development of many of the skills of Citizenship, for example participating in debates and discussions; expressing personal opinions orally; presenting a convincing argument; listening to, and responding to, the arguments of others; researching and planning some action to address a Citizenship issue; negotiating with peers and others and implementing that action; participating in school and community-based Citizenship activities; working with community partners. All of these and more require a somewhat different approach than a conventional test, or even an unconventional test. They may be more difficult to measure than basic elements of subject knowledge, but that is not to say we can ignore them. It is important that we *'measure what we value (for example, showing the ability to participate in group discussions) not just those aspects that are easy to measure (for example knowledge of facts)'* (QCA, 2007).

The use of peer and self-assessment techniques can be a really worthwhile addition to a Citizenship teacher's assessment toolbox. A supportive classroom atmosphere, where students work collaboratively, is an important factor in ensuring the success of this approach. One way of introducing peer assessment to group work is to assign a couple of students the role of 'observer'. Their task is to assess group performance and individual contribution and then report back to the class on the main points of discussion. This requires some time by the teacher to prepare 'observers' to ensure they know what they are looking for. This can be done while the rest of the class moves into their groups, receives and then reads through the task sheet. Observers can be briefed to note down the following:

(Continued)

- Are there any instances of good team working?
- Does anyone take the lead in the group?
- Is everyone being given the chance to contribute?
- Is consensus met and, if so, how?

I find this method to be beneficial in terms of enhancing students' emotional development. It takes confidence and maturity to take a measured and unbiased stance when assessing peers.

For each new unit of work, I produce a checklist of knowledge and skills that students are expected to gain by the conclusion of the unit. Students mark a 'before' and 'after' column which allows them to highlight their initial understanding and competence and then repeat the process at the end of the unit to highlight what they have learned. This is a quick and visual way of plotting progress and gets students to think about their own learning needs. Of course, one has to watch that they aren't just going through the motions with their coloured pencils! To guard against this, I usually follow up the exercise with some whole-class question and answers where those who have marked a section in 'green', indicating that they believe they do understand, offer an explanation to those who have marked it in 'red'.

To accompany group work and particularly role play activities, I always include, where practical, an informal self and peer assessment element. The health warning with this approach is to ensure students don't simply treat this as a tick box exercise. If this approach is to truly enable students to regulate their own learning, they must be of sufficient maturity and given appropriate guidance by the teacher. There is a need to invest some time with classes explaining assessment criteria. For the teacher, it should not be seen merely as a way to cut down on one's marking workload!

At Bradford Academy, the Citizenship department is trialling a new way of working with Year 8 and 9 students. This involves setting an extended piece of work or 'challenge' over a number of lessons, containing various tasks to be completed in small groups. One example is the 'Fairtrade challenge', where Year 8 students are required to produce a poster and Powerpoint presentation to promote Fairtrade, draft a school policy and come up with an enterprise activity to raise awareness of Fairtrade issues among the wider school community.

This way of working promotes core Citizenship skills such as research, enquiry, communication and participation. It also requires students to manage their time efficiently, allocating and prioritizing tasks within their groups. Each 'challenge' contains clearly set out success criteria as well as teacher, self and peer assessment. I have found this approach

(Continued)

to be very successful, giving students a real sense of control and independence. As students get used to working collaboratively, many become adept at assessing their roles within groups and highlighting targets for the next challenge. There are, however, pitfalls to be aware of when using this kind of portfolio work. If you are not careful, completed challenges can just collect dust once completed. Displaying work on walls is one way of helping prolong their life. Perhaps periodic review sessions, using past portfolios, to reinforce learning might also have a place within the context of ongoing assessment.

Andy Thorpe, Citizenship teacher, Bradford Academy

Think for a moment about the way in which you are being assessed (or were assessed) for your own PGCE and QTS. You are assessed not just on your factual knowledge of your subject, but on a range of skills that you demonstrate: your preparation and planning of lessons; your presentations; your classroom management; your facility with ICT and so on. In order to prove those skills, you are required to put together a portfolio of evidence. The name applied to this portfolio (which probably consists of several large ring binders at least) will vary between teacher education institutions; it may be called a Professional Development Portfolio, or an Individual Development Plan, or something similar. In here you might keep samples of work you have done, your own self-evaluations of that work, copies of feedback from observing mentors and tutors, action plans that you will pursue in follow up to that feedback, the results of those action plans and more. In Citizenship Education we are also in the business of teaching and learning skills that do not lend themselves easily to testing by quizzes and examinations, so why not take the model from the PGCE/QTS and encourage your students to prove their skills through the keeping of some kind of learning log and portfolio of evidence?

Perhaps the hardest part of Citizenship assessment is the task of assessing values and attitudes, or more specifically, progress, change and development of values and attitudes, particularly towards controversial issues. On the page opposite, Aashiya Chaus describes one approach to this challenge. Aashiya is a Citizenship teacher at Challenge College, Bradford, a school geographically very close to the location of the Bradford riots of 2001.

I developed this assessment tool with my Year 11 Citizenship class when examining the causes of the Bradford riots. At the start of the topic I gave students a sheet with a pie chart outline on each side. I listed a number of agents whose actions might have triggered the riots, including the BNP (who had announced a plan to march in the city and hold a public meeting), British Asian young people from Bradford (who felt the march should be banned), the local council (in whose premises the meeting was to be held) and the Police (charged with maintaining public order), and asked the students to allocate responsibility for the riots on one pie chart, identifying agents from my list, or others they could think of. Most responses were one dimensional, allocating nearly all the blame to one, or perhaps two, agents; and highly partisan. At the end of the unit of work I asked the students to complete the second pie chart. Most responses now showed that students recognized multiple and complex triggers, and a wider range of agencies sharing the responsibility for the events, including the media and others. Besides demonstrating that learning had taken place, that both knowledge and attitudes had changed, this assessment tool was useful because it did not discriminate against those who would find writing an essay (for example) difficult. All students were able to visualize their learning and understanding.

Aashiya Chaus, Citizenship teacher, Challenge College, Bradford

Once again, we are not pretending to have all the answers here. We simply want to alert you to the issues you will need to consider regarding assessment in Citizenship, to show you some of the ways in which teachers are thinking creatively about these issues, and to encourage you to put your mind to developing new and imaginative assessment strategies of your own.

Assessment of learning in Citizenship

Periodically we may wish to, or we may be required to, make judgements on what learning has been achieved, to make an assessment of learning. As teachers we are expected to make these summative assessments, both to report to parents and to provide data for government 'bean counters'; schools are required to report to the DCSF on the progress of all children, to enable governments to report to the electorate on the success of their educational policies.

Some of our students will be subject to the summative assessments of others through the process of public examinations. The ultimate form of summative assessment is the formal examination at the end of a course of study (the GCSE, or the GCE 'A' level, for example).

Summative assessment consists of making a summary statement of what has been learned, and to what level.

Summative assessment allows us to celebrate achievements; to be able to say 'well done'. Hence we have degree award ceremonies or prizegivings and the like in schools. However, there are 'mixed blessings' from the process of summative assessment and the giving of awards and certificates for students. Fine for those who can celebrate success, but what of those who have not done so well? Nonetheless, parents, potential employers and government expect these procedures to take place.

Note that it is possible for summative assessments to be used in a formative way. A summative assessment at the end of a particular unit of work or project could be used to set targets for an individual, or group of students, for subsequent units/projects. Mock examinations some months prior to the real thing can give students pointers to their areas of strength and weakness, and inform a revision programme, for example.

Assessment and reporting at Key Stage 3; the statutory requirements

From September 2008, changes have been made to the National Curriculum generally, and to Citizenship in particular. One such change has been to bring Citizenship into line with the other National Curriculum subjects, and require schools to report about students' progress at Key Stage 3 based on an eight-point scale; a set of criterion referenced 'levels'. Examples of the attainment targets, or the assessment criteria, for Citizenship at different levels at Key Stage 3 are given below.

Level 1

Pupils can talk about citizenship issues that are suggested to them. They think of questions they would like to ask about these issues and identify who could help them answer these questions. They consider what their opinions are and share their ideas with others. They describe some of the groups and communities they belong to and recognise that people in their communities are different. They begin to describe how needs are different from wants. They take part in some of the decisions that affect them and their communities.

Level 4

Pupils explore a range of sources of information to engage with topical and controversial issues, including where rights compete and conflict.

(Continued)

They identify different and opposing views and can explain their own opinion about what is fair and unfair in different situations. They develop research questions to explore issues and problems and begin to assess the impact of these for individuals and communities. They use what they find out to make informed contributions in debates. They appreciate that there are many diverse groups and communities in the UK and the wider world and use this understanding to explore the communities they belong to. They work with others to plan and undertake a course of action to address significant citizenship issues. They begin to explain different ways in which people can participate in democracy through individual and collective actions and how they can change things in communities and wider society. They show understanding of democracy by making connections with their knowledge and experience of representation and taking action in the local community.

Level 8

Pupils use and apply their detailed knowledge of citizenship issues, problems and events to analyse how these affect groups and communities in different parts of the world. They make connections between information derived from different sources and their own experience to make perceptive observations. They have a detailed understanding of the key citizenship concepts of democracy, justice, rights and responsibilities, identities and diversity, including how these can change over time. They carry out different types of research and hypothesise alternative courses of action, exploring the different implications of each. They put some of the courses of action to the test in their communities and analyse and draw conclusions about the impact and limitations of these. They understand how citizens participate in bringing about change in society through democratic processes and different kinds of action. They ask challenging questions to explore the ways in which justice, laws and governments operate in different places, and the roles citizens can take in shaping society.

'Programme of study for Key Stage 3' (QCA, 2007)

Note that although we therefore have a criterion based model of assessment for the National Curriculum generally, there is an element of norm referencing remaining; because governments will set performance targets for schools which demand that a certain percentage of children in a certain age group will achieve at a certain level.

One of the problems we face as Citizenship teachers is matching the work we do with students, and the assessments we make of their work, to these target levels. Sarah Frost and James Rawling, Citizenship teachers at Kettlethorpe High School, Wakefield, have deconstructed the statements in the levels, and then mapped them against the key knowledge and skills areas of the Citizenship curriculum. Again, we supply an example of their mapping below.

Figure 7.2 Mapping target levels to Citizenship knowledge and skills

Level	Knowledge and understanding	Research and critical thinking	Communication	Taking informed and responsible action
8	You can ask challenging questions to explore justice and law. You can evaluate the impact and limitations of policies on communities. You can debate challenging questions.	You apply your detailed knowledge of issues to analyse how these affect different communities around the world. You can make connections between information from different sources.	You use your own experiences in order to make perceptive observations and coherent arguments.	You can carry out some courses of action in your community and analyse and draw conclusions about the limitations of these.
5	You can identify the contributions of different cultures to society. You show knowledge of the operation of the criminal justice system and political system in the UK.	You recognize and investigate issues that affect people. You can answer questions using different information.	You can communicate your argument clearly, supporting your opinion. You can take part in activities involving voting and campaigning.	You identify something that could be changed and plan some action. You take part in decision making.
3	You can identify different kinds of rights and begin to recognize some features of democracy.	You recognize and investigate issues that affect people. You can answer questions using different information.	You can present your ideas to others.	You identify something that could be changed and plan some action. You take part in decision making.

A greater problem is explaining, and making accessible, the levels to the students who are being judged by them. Sarah and James have made a good start on that task also, designing a 'level ladder' which may be posted on classroom walls and which students may reference, to see where they are now, and what they will need to do to move on to the next level. We would argue that this tool shifts the assessment process in the direction of ipsative assessment, allowing teachers and students to monitor their progress not just against the level criteria, but against their own past performance.

Figure 7.3 Are *you* climbing the level ladder?

Knowledge and Understanding

Level 8

You can ask challenging questions to explore justice and law. You can evaluate the impact and limitations of policies on communities. You can debate challenging questions.

Level 7

You can analyse the reason for diversity in the UK. You can evaluate the roles of citizens in shaping decisions. You can compare the role of citizens in the UK with those in other countries and illustrate strengths and weaknesses of different types of government.

Level 6

You understand the complexity of identities and diversity in communities. You can explain how different rights need to be protected, supported and balanced. You compare the UK system of government to other countries.

Level 5

You can identify the contributions of different cultures to society. You show knowledge of the operation of the criminal justice system and political system in the UK.

Level 4

You appreciate there are diverse groups in the UK and world. You can explain different ways for participating in democracy.

Level 3

You can identify different kinds of rights and begin to recognize some features of democracy.

Communication

Level 8

You use your own experiences in order to make perceptive observations and coherent arguments.

Level 7

You can question assumptions and your own views as a result of informed debate and examination of evidence. You can argue persuasively and represent the views of others.

Level 6

You can develop informed arguments, taking account of different viewpoints. You use your findings to present a persuasive argument, supported with evidence.

Level 5

You can communicate your argument clearly, supporting your opinion. You can take part in activities involving voting and campaigning.

Level 4

You can identify different views and explain your own opinion. You can use what you have found out to make informed contributions to debates.

Level 3

You can present your ideas to others.

Level 8

You apply your detailed knowledge of issues to analyse how these affect different communities around the world. You can make connections between information from different sources.

Level 7

You can explore the origin of a range of opinions, including your own. You confidently use different research strategies and different sources.

Level 6

You are aware of a variety of opinions on different issues. You can interpret information and assess it for validity and bias.

Level 5

You can discuss and debate issues. You can use a variety of sources to research and draw some conclusions.

Level 4

Using research questions, you can explore issues, using a range of sources and assess the impact of these on people.

Level 3

You recognize and investigate issues that affect people. You can answer questions using different information.

Research and Critical Thinking

Level 8

You can carry out some courses of action in your community and analyse and draw conclusions about the limitations of these.

Level 7

You work with others to initiate, negotiate, plan and carry out action in the local and wider community to bring about change.

Level 6

You can negotiate your role and plan and undertake action with others. You can reflect on your success in improving the community.

Level 5

You work with others from the community to negotiate, plan and carry out action to make a difference to others. You can explain the impact of your actions.

Level 4

You work with others to plan and undertake action that will address citizenship issues.

Level 3

You identify something that could be changed and plan some action. You take part in decision making.

Informed and Responsible Action

Public examinations in Citizenship: GCSE and GCE

For many beginning teachers the structure of the public examination system is bewildering, so let us begin by attempting to make some sense of it. Some years ago the government set up the Qualifications and Curriculum Authority (QCA) to oversee a national framework of public examinations. Essentially, QCA established a set of rules and specifications (which it periodically revises) for different levels of examination, and for each subject. Individual examination boards (such as AQA, Edexcel and OCR), which are regulated by QCA, then write and publish syllabuses and examination papers (after approval by QCA, which checks to see that they meet their specifications) and offer these to schools.

Examination boards are businesses that earn an income from 'selling' qualifications. Individual schools 'buy' examinations from the boards. The schools make decisions about which examinations they wish to prepare students for, and register with one or more of the boards. The boards provide the schools with copies of the exam syllabus, and all the rules and regulations; at the appropriate time they provide examination papers and arrange for these to be marked; and they communicate results to the schools and their students in due course. Schools pay a fee to register with an examination board, and a per capita fee for each student they enter for the examination.

Essentially there is a market for examinations. The schools are free to purchase from whichever provider they prefer. Choices may be made on financial grounds; it is cheaper for the school to buy all its examinations from one board, because then they will pay only one registration fee. Historically, there were rather more examination boards than there are today; as in every other business there have been takeovers and mergers. In the past, many examination boards were regionally based, and most schools bought examinations from their local provider. Even today, inertia means that some schools still do business with the successor organizations to those local boards.

Even though all the syllabi and examinations in a particular subject, at a particular level, must meet the QCA specifications, it still allows for some differentiation between the products on offer. In the end (subject to the internal politics of the school) it is normally the Head of Department for a subject who decides which examination to enter his/her students for; so in a few years' time, or sooner, it may be you who is making these decisions for Citizenship in your school.

Teachers may feel that a particular board's examination may suit their students (or the way they like to teach). The structure of the exam, the topics on which questions are asked, the way those questions are asked (and the way students are expected to answer) vary. Some teachers may consider the coursework implications, and whether they feel they can provide the opportunities to do coursework that the different boards demand. Some teachers might consider which coursework requirements mean less work for them personally, and make decisions on that, rather selfish, basis (we know who you are, and we know where you live). Perhaps less rationally, different teachers may perceive different exams as being easier or harder to pass (teachers avidly study the pass rates, and the proportion of students earning higher grades, from the different boards). In reality, this is probably like trying to pick the winner of the Grand National, or having a 'secret formula' that will guarantee winning the National Lottery (just you wait and see – one day!).

We have somewhat mixed feelings about the growth in examinations and credentialization on Citizenship. We are, after all, citizens by right, not by examination. We have the right to participate, to vote, to express an opinion and so much more, irrespective of whether or not we pass an examination in some subject called Citizenship. The purpose of Citizenship Education is to enable us to use our rights more effectively and powerfully; not simply to acquire a piece of paper that says we are 'qualified' in Citizenship. These feelings are shared by many others, including Tony Breslin of the Citizenship Foundation: *'Examining Citizenship, in the curriculum or elsewhere, is . . . a contentious exercise. "Failing" in Citizenship carries a different baggage than probably any other subject and the recent launch of Citizenship . . . "tests" for newcomers to the UK have served to emphasise the following: Citizenship as exclusive rather than inclusive; Citizenship as nationality rather than empowerment; Citizenship as legal status rather than political process. Indeed, the very process of "assessing" Citizenship seems to transfer it from a process to a status, from an activity to a grade. In short, assessing Citizenship seems to go against the grain of what active, effective, Citizenship is'* (Breslin, 2006).

In many schools, when Citizenship programmes of study were introduced, decisions were initially made that this would be a non-examined subject. That was good, in that it gave outstanding Citizenship teachers scope to design a Citizenship programme that addressed the interests and needs of the students they worked with. It allowed topical controversial issues to be discussed at the very moment they were in the public eye (rather than according to some predetermined timetable). However, it also gave some of the weaker conscripts to Citizenship teaching, in those schools where the subject was taught by non-specialists, often in 'form period', the leeway to neglect the subject.

More importantly, the lack of examinations and testing gave students the notion that this new subject was unimportant. Unfortunately, in the eyes of students brought up in a culture of constant testing (SATS, GCSEs, etc.), important things are tested and examined. Examination confers validity/credibility, not only in the eyes of students, but in those of their parents and our peers in the staffroom, specialists in other subjects. The good news for us as Citizenship teachers is that this credentialization of the subject should improve our job prospects; schools are less likely to leave examination classes to non-specialists, and provided we do not become obsessed with 'teaching to the test' we have the opportunity to develop meaningful, and empowering, Citizenship Education programmes for our students.

GCSE Citizenship; short and full courses

From September 2003 QCA provided for a short-course GCSE in Citizenship studies (essentially half a GCSE), and syllabi and examinations were made available by AQA, Edexcel and OCR. The essential format of all three examination papers is similar. The examinations begin with a series of short answer questions to test factual knowledge and understanding. There follows a data analysis section: text passages, graphs or tables of figures, photographs or other visual material, followed by a series of questions of staged levels of difficulty (the earlier questions testing whether the data was understood, the later ones testing the ability to argue a case from the evidence provided by the data and the students' own knowledge). As part of the GCSE short course, students are expected to take part in active citizenship projects or community work. The third section of the examination paper invites them to reflect on this work, their role in the activity, the steps they took to achieve the end result, the difficulties they encountered and what they would do differently next time. Finally there is what amounts to a short essay section, offering a limited choice of topics to write about, with some guidance about issues that might be considered, and inviting students to demonstrate their ability to see, and argue, both sides of a debate and reach a reasoned conclusion; demonstrating skills of analysis, criticism and synthesis.

From September 2009 (for first examination in Summer 2011) a full-course GCSE will be made available. At the time of writing, the examination boards had prepared draft specifications for the new examinations, but were awaiting their final approval by QCA. Full specifications, and sample examination papers, are downloadable from the websites of the examinations boards. Details of the web addresses are provided in the final chapter of this book. For the moment it seems that the examination boards will continue to offer the short courses (or modified versions of them) alongside the new specifications. The long-term survival of the short courses is likely to depend, however, on market forces. If most schools switch to the full awards, the short courses may be phased out.

GCE 'AS' and 'A2' examinations

For some years AQA have offered an AS syllabus entitled Social Sciences (Citizenship). That is set to disappear as QCA have now approved a brand new AS and A2 programme in Citizenship Studies. At the time of writing, only AQA have produced a specification for these courses and examinations; this is available for teaching from September 2008 with first examinations in 2009 (AS) and 2010 (A2). Full details of the specification are available on the AQA website. Perhaps the most interesting aspect of the new specification (and indeed of the new full course GCSE specifications) is that it maintains the requirement to actually undertake some form of active citizenship work, and offer a critical evaluation of this, distinguishing Citizenship from many other AS/A2 courses.

Summary

In this chapter we have endeavoured to give you an awareness of the statutory requirements for assessment in Citizenship, together with some practical suggestions, and case study examples, of how such assessment might be managed. We have also offered an overview of the public examination process, and examinations in Citizenship in particular. Most importantly, we hope we have raised your awareness of the problematic and contentious nature of assessment in general, and in Citizenship specifically; enough we hope to stimulate you once again to think, read more widely and critically reflect on your current and future assessment practice.

Continued professional development in Citizenship

8

Teachers never stop learning. Every time they teach a lesson they learn something about how to communicate a concept, how to make a resource work better or how to manage a particular situation or student. Constant in-built reflection, both on what you are doing and why, is at the core of becoming, and staying, an effective teacher. This is particularly true in Citizenship, where ideas about what works are developing, and even what should be taught is open to debate.

However, outside input, and support from a wider Citizenship community, is important too. As a newly qualified teacher, you may find yourself as the only trained Citizenship teacher in a school. Or, like Carrie Sharman who reflects on her experience below, you may find yourself head of a Citizenship department early in your career. (We can tell you many stories like Carrie's, but suffice it to say that of the graduates from one Citizenship PGCE course in 2004/2005, of the 12 who decided to enter Citizenship teaching, five were Citizenship Co-ordinator or Head of Department in their schools within two years, and others have become so since.) Even if you are lucky enough to work in a well-established department, taking time to train on new technology, learn from those with different experiences, or strengthen subject knowledge, helps keep you inspired.

Like many students who gain their PGCE in Citizenship, I did not initially find work as a Citizenship teacher, but as a 'Teacher of Psychology and Citizenship'. The Citizenship department at the time was very underdeveloped, but despite needing a lot of TLC the fortnightly delivery did not justify a full-time teacher. Straight after my NQT year I was appointed to Key Stage 4 coordinator and a year later to Head of Citizenship. This made me the youngest Head of Department in the school, and the one with the least teaching experience.

Many Citizenship teachers find that their career progression is speedy due to it being a relatively new subject. However, the exciting career

(Continued)

development opportunities must be balanced with the vast task of managing a department – and in some cases setting one up from scratch!

At Twyford High School, Citizenship is taught once fortnightly in Key Stage 3. This means that I have regularly ended up teaching whole year groups of students. Setting homework and working out when to collect in books for marking has therefore become a military operation. At Twyford students get a sheet at the start of the year which contains all their homework tasks and the deadlines. One in three times I will mark their books myself, the other occasions we will peer mark or self-mark in the lesson time.

Working out your own systems for keeping organized is all part of being a teacher but being a Head of Department means feeling these things more acutely. However, being too controlling about departmental systems leads to teachers losing ownership and motivation for the subject. I have learned to balance how prescriptive I am. Encouraging staff to do their own problem solving leads to them having more initiative and interest in the department. Leading in a democratic way also feeds into teachers' management of their classrooms, and gets them in touch with the ethos of the subject.

It is common that the staff who form the Citizenship department are not full-time members, but 'borrowed' from other departments to teach one period of Citizenship here and there. Often these staff are seconded from related departments like RE, History, Geography, but not always! Helping staff to feel professionally confident in the subject is important for their enjoyment and confidence in the classroom. Exploiting overlaps between different subjects can also be beneficial; for example the English department may run a debate club at which they would be happy to discuss controversial current affairs issues.

Last year, at the end of my third year of teaching, I was appointed as an Advanced Skills Teacher, which means that the London Borough of Ealing can 'loan' me to other schools in the borough for one day a week to help develop their own departments. Being a Head of Citizenship is a challenge but having the opportunity to carve out the department's identity has been incredibly rewarding and helped my professional development enormously.

Carrie Sharman, Head of Citizenship and Ealing borough AST,
Twyford High School

In this book, we have tried to provide you with a taste of the subject, and lots of food for thought. But what we have written is really just a start. This chapter contains a huge number of places where you can go for more. It includes websites and organizations as well as specific books. Some offer advice for teachers, or training opportunities; others are good sources of teaching activities and resources. We have done our best to describe for you what each organization we list can offer teachers. Better still, some organizations have agreed to explain their work to you in their own words.

Action Aid
www.actionaid.org.uk
Action Aid provide a range of resources to support the teaching of the global dimension, including a team of visiting speakers and 'Get Global!', a guide for teachers on how to facilitate and assess active global citizenship. They also have a free new DVD-based resource launched in 2008 called 'Power Down', which looks at sustainability issues for schools.

Amnesty International
www.amnesty.org.uk
A core part of Amnesty's work is promoting awareness of human rights through educational materials for use at school, college and home. This website provides information on teaching resources, a teacher's network and visiting speakers. You'll remember we discussed Citizenship Education itself as a controversial issue? Here's just one example. We've heard that some Roman Catholic schools have banned teachers from using the resources mentioned here, and banned students from setting up Amnesty groups in school, because Amnesty's views on a woman's right to choose to have an abortion contradict Roman Catholic teaching.

AQA
www.aqa.org.uk
UK awarding body for GCEs, GCSEs and other exams, offering Citizenship short course and AS/A2, and draft specifications for a full GCSE.

Association for Citizenship Teaching (ACT)
www.teachingcitizenship.org.uk
The association exists to further the aims of Citizenship teaching and learning, connecting teachers to regional and national networks,

offering training, support and advice. The association publishes a termly journal, *Teaching Citizenship*; a monthly e-newsletter with events, conferences and teaching resources; and holds an annual conference in the summer term.

BBC

http://news.bbc.co.uk/cbbcnews – Newsround, the news programme for young people includes a section for teachers.

www.bbc.co.uk/schools – BBC Schools, accessible information on a huge range of topics. Add citizenx/ for their site dedicated to Citizenship issues, with games and activities for students and lesson plans for teachers.

British Council

www.britishcouncil.org

The British Council is the UK's international organization for educational opportunities and cultural relations, aiming to build mutually beneficial relationships between people in the UK and other countries. The organization offers UK teachers professional development opportunities overseas, and supports international work in schools (through student exchanges, partnerships and joint projects with schools in other countries, and the magazine *Learning World*). The British Council, funded by DfID and working with a number of partners, delivers the 'Global School Partnerships' programme. This programme offers advice, guidance, grants and professional development opportunities for schools committed to using their link as a means of developing a global dimension within the curriculum.

British Red Cross

www.redcross.org.uk

As part of their work helping people in crisis, the British Red Cross produce educational resources that promote humanitarian values, human dignity and awareness of the laws of war.

> **Nadia Robinson is the project manager for British Red Cross education.**
> **The online project supplies lesson plans, quick ideas, photo resources**
> **and background briefings for teachers. Visitors to www.redcross.org.**
> **uk/education can download free materials, complete with curriculum**
> **links, and subscribe to a mailing list.**
>
> Many teachers know us best for the fortnightly 'news think!' we send
> throughout the school year. Each bulletin neatly summarizes

(Continued)

four current news stories and adds questions and discussion ideas for classroom use. Teachers use them in a variety of ways: discussions at tutor time; for cover lessons; or as the basis for larger citizenship projects.

We were pleased when international humanitarian law was explicitly mentioned in the Citizenship curriculum in England – the Red Cross charter tasks us with promoting education on it. More generally, humanity is at the core of all the materials.

When we launched the project back in 2005, assembly planning was an area teachers seemed to want resources for. We also committed to providing lesson plans with a strong and sometimes surprising narrative. They help students develop their understanding of different viewpoints, think through available options and appreciate other people's circumstances. The 'class acts' challenge preconceptions and raise difficult dilemmas. But none are invented. They are all genuine incidents based on real people.

The 'ten-minute briefings' were designed to fill a gap in teachers' knowledge and confidence in exploring specialist topics. Feedback suggests they are used as teaching resources in their own right. So we always include suggestions for further activities along with the factual briefing.

Britkid

www.britkid.org

A website about race, racism and growing up in Britain, based on the lives of nine young people living in 'Britchester'. Aimed at young people who do not live or go to school in areas which are ethnically mixed.

Changemakers

www.changemakers.org.uk

Changemakers is an independent charity and social enterprise which enables young people aged 4–25 to make a positive and continuing contribution to society.

Christian Aid

http://learn.christianaid.org.uk

Christian Aid, agency of the churches in the UK and Ireland, has an online catalogue of downloadable or easy-to-order resources, for assemblies and the classroom (including a number of role plays).

citizED

www.citized.info

citizED is an organization funded by the Training and Development Agency for Schools (TDA). It is a collaboration within higher education for all providers of initial teacher education in England. citizED is organized principally around teacher education in primary, secondary, cross-curricular, post-16 and community involvement contexts with outputs in the form of conferences, seminars, workshops, research papers and practical resources for teaching. An international journal of citizenship and teacher education was launched by citizED in July 2005.

Citizenship Foundation

www.citizenshipfoundation.org.uk

The Citizenship Foundation is an independent education and participation charity that exists to encourage and enable individuals to play an effective role in democratic society. The foundation produces resources for teachers and students, many of which are free, and run a number of programmes including:

- G-Nation: a schools-based programme providing teachers with free resources that promote charitable activity, decision making and reflection.
- Diversity and Dialogue: aims to build better understanding between young people from different faiths and backgrounds by supporting a UK-wide network of interfaith, intercultural and social cohesion initiatives.
- Go-Givers: a programme for primary schools promoting ideas of charity and empathy.
- Citizenship Manifestos: aims to bring coherence and structure to secondary Citizenship Education through supporting schools to create citizenship manifestos.
- Twinning: a scheme twinning lawyers and schools for a programme of workshops facilitated by trainee or qualified solicitors.
- Youth Act: supporting groups of young people who want to achieve change in their school, youth club or community.

The Citizenship Foundation also runs a number of competitions including:

- Bar National Mock Trial: young people from all over Britain take part in a criminal mock trial in a real court.

- Magistrates' Court Mock Trial: school teams go head to head in local Magistrates' Courts.
- National Youth Parliament: young people compete by creating a video of a mock parliamentary session.

The Citizenship Foundation produce:

Jarvis, R. and Thorpe, T. (2006), *Inside Britain: A Guide to the UK Constitution*. London: Hodder Education.

Thorpe, T. (ed.) (2007), *Young Citizen's Passport, England and Wales: 12th edition*. London: Hodder Education.

CSV

www.csv.org.uk

CSV supports volunteers and works with schools to provide opportunities for young people to make a difference in their local communities.

Demgames

www.demgames.org

Demgames provides online interactive games around local democracy issues, for example students can play at being a local councillor.

Department for Children, Schools and Families

www.dcsf.gov.uk

The DCSF leads work across government to improve outcomes for children, including work on children's health and child poverty.

Development Education Association

www.dea.org.uk

DEA is an education charity that promotes global learning, with a national network of member organizations and supporters who share their commitment to education for a just and sustainable world. DEA works to influence global learning policy; to enable the improvement of educational practice; and to raise the profile of global learning. Contact them to find out about your local Development Education Centre.

**Sandy Betlem is Schools' Work Coordinator at Norfolk Education &
Action for Development, a member of the DEA.**

If you need help with delivering the global dimension in the Citizenship
curriculum then a good way to start is by contacting your local
Development Education Centre. There are over 40 DECs in the UK.
Some are small, some are big, some are new and some are long
established (like NEAD), but they are all committed to raising the
profile of global issues and encouraging positive local action for
global change. They promote the idea that we are all part of an
interdependent global society, and that we have a responsibility to
contribute to the creation of a fairer, safer, healthier, sustainable and
more cohesive world.

Each DEC defines its own areas of work in response to local
needs and enquiries, but most work with schools, teachers and local
authorities to enrich the curriculum. DECs can provide invaluable
information and advice about global issues, and many have resource
libraries or sell quality teaching resources. Some have staff available
to come into your school to inform and enable your students to take
action on a range of global issues. Many DECs also have strong links
with communities in the global south.

All DECs aim to promote effective Development Education which:

- explores the links between people living in the 'developed'
  countries of the North with those of the 'developing' South,
  enabling people to understand the links between their own lives
  and those of people throughout the world
- increases understanding of the economic, social, political and
  environmental forces which shape our lives
- develops the skills, attitudes and values that enable people to
  work individually or together to take action to bring about change
  and take control of their own lives
- works towards achieving a more just and a more sustainable world
  in which power and resources are more equitably shared

To find your nearest DEC go to www.dea.org.uk

Edexcel
www.edexcel.org.uk
An awarding body offering short-course GCSE and draft specifications
for a full GCSE.

The Electoral Commission

www.electoralcommission.org.uk
www.dopolitics.org.uk

Part of the Electoral Commission's role is to encourage people to get involved in democracy, and their Do Politics Centre is a resource hub for anyone trying to do the same. Their *Democracy Cookbook*, providing both the ingredients and recipes to explain how our democracy works, is particularly well known.

UK Office of the European Parliament

www.europarl.org.uk/education

Order a free issues-based pack aimed at promoting discussion about the function of the EU and its Parliament and the implications of EU membership.

Global Dimension

www.globaldimension.org.uk

This website from DfID is a helpful guide to books, films, posters and websites with a global dimension.

Global Gateway

www.globalgateway.org.uk

The DCSF Global Gateway provides quick access to comprehensive information on how to develop an international dimension to education. The website is managed and hosted by the British Council.

Hansard Society

www.hansardsociety.org.uk

The Hansard Society's Citizenship Education Programme works with young people through schools and colleges to educate and inform them about parliamentary democracy. It aims to involve young people in participatory democratic activities, through teaching resources, the HeadsUp site (www.headsup.org.uk – a forum where young people can debate political issues and current affairs), and the Y Vote Mock Elections (see separate entry).

Headliners

www.headliners.org

Headliners is a UK-wide news agency producing news, features and comment by young people. Extensive story library with articles on a range of issues.

I'm a councillor, get me out of here

www.bigvote.org.uk

'I'm a councillor, get me out of here' is a project that allows students to talk to their local councillor over the internet during local democracy week, in October.

Institute for Citizenship

www.citizen.org.uk

The Institute for Citizenship is a charity which aims to promote informed, active citizenship and greater participation in democracy and society through a combination of community projects, research, education, discussion and debate. The institute produces a range of Citizenship Education resources for teachers and students, many of which are available to download free from their website.

Just Business

www.jusbiz.org

Just Business provides information and activities about global and ethical issues for students and teachers of Business Studies and Economics, but useful for teachers of Citizenship too. The site includes free, downloadable role play games and other resources.

Learning and Skills Network

www.post16citizenship.org

The Learning and Skills Network has a major responsibility for post-16 education and has produced a wide range of glossy high quality resources for post-16 Citizenship teaching, all of which are available free of charge and many of which are adaptable for Key Stage 4. Titles include: *Agree to Disagree: Citizenship and Controversial Issues*; *We all Came here from Somewhere: Diversity, Identities and Citizenship*; *Getting the Show on the Road: Skills for Planning and Running Citizenship Events*; and *Get Up, Stand Up: Citizenship Through Music*. A comprehensive list is available on the website, and new resources are constantly added. It is possible to place yourself on the LSN emailing service to receive information about their latest publications, and continuing professional development opportunities for Citizenship teachers.

Making Sense of Citizenship *(Ted Huddleston and David Kerr, eds)*

This book, developed by the Citizenship Foundation and ACT, is a handbook for continuing professional development in Citizenship.

It is published by Hodder Murray (2006) and is available at www. hoddereducation.co.uk.

Model United Nations
www.una.org.uk/mun
This website, from the United Nations Association of the UK, aims to support all those organizing and taking part in Model UN events

mySociety
www.mysociety.org
mySociety builds websites that give people simple, tangible benefits in the civic and community aspects of their lives, including:
www.theyworkforyou.com – Lets you know what your MP is doing in their role as your representative.
www.writetothem.com – This website gives you details of your local, national and EU representatives. It enables you to send them a letter via email, and gives lots of good advice about the most effective way of getting your point across to them.

National Curricula
England: You can access the National Curriculum at the site below, as well as advice on organizing, developing and evaluating your curriculum and case studies of good practice: http://curriculum.qca. org.uk.

Scotland: The Citizenship pages of the 'Learning and Teaching Scotland' website detail the Scottish approach to Citizenship Education: www.ltscotland.org.uk/citizenship.

Wales: The *Personal and Social Education Framework for 7 to 19-year-olds in Wales*, part of the Welsh National Curriculum, addresses many of the themes of Citizenship Education. You can download it at:
http://new.wales.gov.uk/dcells/publications/curriculum_
and_assessment/arevisedcurriculumforwales/
personalandsocialeducation/PSE_Framework_WEB_(E).
pdf?lang=en

OCR
www.ocr.org.uk
Awarding body offering short-course Citizenship GCSE, and draft specifications for a full GCSE.

Ofsted – the Office for Standards in Education, Children's Services and Skills

www.ofsted.gov.uk

Ofsted's website includes their inspection reports for specific schools and other organizations, and a searchable database of recommendations and wider reports, including those on the state of Citizenship provision in the UK. The key Ofsted document that all Citizenship teachers need to read is *Towards Consensus?*, 2006. It will prove invaluable when you seek to improve Citizenship provision in your school and you need to persuade senior management to support you.

Oxfam

www.oxfam.org.uk/education

www.oxfam.org.uk/generationwhy

Oxfam Education offers a huge range of ideas, resources and support for developing the global dimension in the classroom and the whole school. Their 'generation why' website includes lots of active citizenship ideas for young people.

Parliament's Education Service

www.parliament.uk/education

www.explore.parliament.uk

Parliament's Education Service works with schools and Members of both Houses of Parliament to support young people in developing their understanding of Parliament and democracy.

Claire O'Neill is the Education Outreach Manager at the Education Service, Houses of Parliament.

We work to:

- Inform young people about the role, work and history of Parliament through educational visits, tours, publications and outreach
- Engage young people to understand the relevance of Parliament and democracy today through active learning
- Empower young people to get involved by equipping them with the knowledge and skills to take part

To achieve this, we offer resources and support for students and teachers including:

(Continued)

- Visits – an exciting range of themed workshops and tours for school visits, including, where possible, a questions and answers session with the school's MP
- Education Outreach – our outreach programme focuses on training to equip teachers, student teachers and other education practitioners with ideas, activities and resources that can be used to teach young people about the work and role of Parliament
- Teaching resources – online, print and DVD classroom resources, and even video-conferencing on the work of Parliament

Our services are free and have been designed to support the political literacy and Citizenship Education requirements of the National Curriculum in the United Kingdom.

Qualifications and Curriculum Authority

www.qca.org.uk

QCA is the regulatory body for public examinations and publicly funded qualifications including the curriculum for the under-5s, the National Curriculum and GCSEs.

The Red Box

www.redbox.gov.uk

This site gives access to information about how the government raises money through taxation, and spends these funds on services such as health care and education. There is a teacher's guide and a range of interactive games for young people of different ages, involving budgeting and prioritizing spending; an important aspect of how the economy functions.

Save the Children

www.savethechildren.org.uk

Save the Children's Education Unit provides a range of free and priced resources for teachers and youth workers promoting global child rights education.

School Councils UK

www.schoolcouncils.org

A charity which offers resources, training and support to help schools develop their school councils.

Schools Linking Network

www.schoolslinkingnetwork.org.uk

The Schools Linking Network is based in Bradford, working with 100 local schools, but they are currently embarking on a national programme to support other local authorities across the UK to establish sustainable and effective linking programmes.

Angie Kotler and Lee Scholtz are Strategic Director and Secondary Adviser at Schools Linking Network

The Schools Linking Project began in late 2001 and grew out of two seemingly separate concerns: first, that many children were underachieving in our primary schools particularly in Key Stage 2, and secondly, that after the riots in the summer of 2001 and the events of 9/11, there was a growing unease about separation between different ethnic groups, both within, but mainly between, many of our schools in Bradford.

Thinking about these two issues, it became increasingly clear that the two were not at all disconnected: in fact we believed and still do believe that there is a fundamental link between them. Underachievement of many young people, especially those from some ethnic minorities and poorer white boys, is inextricably linked to disaffection or disengagement, and separation in communities can only exacerbate feelings of isolation and disengagement.

So the Linking Project developed out of an idea that it might be possible to address the two concerns by bringing together groups of children from different ethnic backgrounds, to work on issues that affect them all and give them real opportunities for exploration, discussion and expression of their perspectives on their lives in this very confusing and increasingly volatile world.

The very first link was between two Year 6 classes, one from a suburban school with Beacon status for writing and a 99% white population, and the other from an inner city primary school with Beacon status for inclusion and a 99% Pakistani population. Innovative drama developed with the two classes working together on themes such as immigration, growing up and leaving home, and building bridges between communities. With the stimulus and support of Cartwright Hall Art Gallery, the children also made multi-faith signs for prayer rooms in public places, painted portraits of themselves as they wanted to be seen and produced a beautiful banner of linking-panels as a symbol of their relationship.

We looked initially at the Key Stage 2 curriculum and how it could be opened up to include different perspectives and we kept communication as our main focus – within classrooms, between

(Continued)

schools, to other audiences. Crucially, we found that creativity was fundamental to creating the space for dialogue to occur. After a few short months these children told us that this work was important, that all children should have the chance to meet those from different backgrounds, that we wouldn't have riots if we did more of this. Not only that, they had the confidence to talk to the Home Office and to perform their drama in public in front of large audiences; they wrote letters and newspaper articles, appeared on local television and generally convinced everyone that by working together they were growing in confidence as young citizens of Bradford. This work really came from their hearts. It provided clear evidence that engaging children in issues that are directly relevant to their lives is not only worthwhile but essential. This is what Citizenship Education is about.

Now that we work with both primary and secondary schools we find the same challenges and the same desires among young people of all ages: to have the freedom to explore both who they are and who the people around them are. They do not want to live in ignorance and fear or be prey to 'received wisdom' – they want the means to be able to both find out for themselves and to form their own opinions. A recent 'Question Time' event that we held on the question of Britishness (part of which was shown in a *Panorama* documentary), showed that young people take this issue seriously and realize that there are no easy answers.

Seven years on, the context we are working in has only increased the imperative for this work. Schools are under growing pressure not only to help their students to achieve academically, but also prepare them for life in a complex, diverse and global society. The new duty on schools to contribute to community cohesion poses fresh challenges for many. On the basis of the successful work in Bradford, we were asked to develop a national network to support schools to meet this challenge. Just as the Schools Linking Project in Bradford started with the view that cohesion and achievement are inextricably linked, so the work of the Schools Linking Network continues to grow and evolve, within the ethos and curriculum of schools across England, in order to achieve these twin aims.

TeacherNet

www.teachernet.gov.uk

TeacherNet is a site developed by the Department for Children, Schools and Families, as a resource to support the education profession. You can find information about teaching and learning (including teaching resources), whole-school issues, management, professional development and educational research. New material is being added all the time. The Sustainable Schools section (www.teachernet.gov.uk/sustainableschools) offers guidance on how to embed the principles of sustainable development into the heart of school life.

Training and Development Agency for Schools
www.tda.gov.uk
The Training and Development Agency for Schools (TDA) is the national agency responsible for the training and development of the school workforce – you will know them from your QTS skills tests.

UK Youth Parliament
www.ukyouthparliament.org.uk
UKYP elections take place each year, in every part of the UK: each LEA representing a UKYP constituency. There are currently 500 elected MYPs (Members of Youth Parliament) who meet together regularly at a regional level, to organize campaigns, projects and events and to identify common issues of concern.

UNICEF
www.unicef.org.uk
A variety of fully photocopiable resources, lesson plans and activities can be downloaded free from this website, many related to children's rights. Contains links to Youth Voice, and World Explorers – UNICEF websites for young people.

United Nations Cyberschoolbus
www.un.org/cyberschoolbus
Information about the United Nations and games, activities and lesson ideas on global issues.

War on Want
www.waronwant.org
War on Want campaigns for human rights and against the root causes of global poverty, inequality and injustice. Their website provides useful reports and campaigning materials.

We are what we do
www.wearewhatwedo.org
We are what we do aims to inspire people to take small everyday actions to change the world. Includes resources for schools.

Y Vote Mock Elections

www.mockelections.co.uk

Y Vote Mock Elections supports schools to run mock elections, with the aim of actively engaging students with the political, social and moral issues of the world around them by giving them the opportunity to stand as party candidates, speech writers and canvassers in a mock election.

Bibliography

Advisory Group on Citizenship (1998), *Education for Citizenship and the Teaching of Democracy in Schools*. London: QCA.

Ajegbo, K. (2007), *Diversity and Citizenship Curriculum Review*. London: DfES.

Ash, R. (2007), *Top Ten of Everything 2008*. London: Hamlyn.

Black, P. and William, D. (1998), *Inside the Black Box: Raising Standards Through Classroom Assessment*. London: King's College.

Black, P., Harrison, C., Lee, C., Marshall, B. and William, D. (2002), *Working Inside the Black Box: Assessment for Learning in the Classroom*. London: King's College.

Breslin, T. (2006), 'Calling Citizenship to account: issues of assessment and progression', in Breslin, T. and Dufour, B. (2006), *Developing Citizens*. London: Hodder Murray, pp. 320–30.

Brown, K. (2006), 'School linking and teaching and learning Global Citizenship'. Commissioned research article published online by CitizED: www.citized.info.

Brown, K. (2008), *How Green is Your Class? Over 50 Ways Young People can Make a Difference*. London: Continuum.

Cameron, J. and Fairbrass, S. (2004), 'From development awareness to enabling effective support: the changing profile of Development Education in England'. *Journal of International Development*, 16, 729–40.

Cantle, T., Kaur, D., Athar, M., Dallison, C., Wiggans, A. and Joshua, H. (2006), *Challenging Local Communities to Change Oldham*. Coventry: Institute of Community Cohesion.

Capel, S., Leask, M. and Turner, T. (2005), *Learning to Teach in the Secondary School. A Companion to School Experience*. London: Routledge.

Chambers, R. (2002), *Participatory Workshops. A Sourcebook of 21 Sets of Ideas and Activities*. London: Earthscan Publications.

Clarke, F. (2002), 'Democracy has to be lived to be learned'. *The Times Education Supplement*, 20/10/2002.

Department for Children, Schools and Families (2007), *Guidance on the Duty to Promote Community Cohesion*. London: DCSF.

Department for Education and Skills (2004), *Every Child Matters: Change for Children in Schools*. London: DfES.

Department for Education and Skills (2006), *Sustainable Schools for Pupils, Communities and the Environment; Delivering UK*

Sustainable Development Strategy. London: DfES.

Department for International Development/Department for Education and Skills (2005), *Developing the Global Dimension in the School Curriculum.* London: DfES.

Fairbrass, S. (2004), 'The global in the local'. *The Development Education Journal*, 11.1, 32–3.

Freire, P. (1970), *Pedagogy of the Oppressed.* London: Penguin.

Gardner, H. (2006), *Multiple Intelligences: New Horizons.* New York: Basic Books.

Gearon, L. (ed.) (2003), *Learning to Teach Citizenship in the Secondary School: A Companion for the Student Teacher of Citizenship.* London: Routledge.

Hansen, S. and Jensen, J. (1971), *The Little Red School Book.* London: Stage One Books.

Hart, R. (1992), *Children's Participation: From Tokenism to Citizenship.* Florence: Innocenti Essays No 4. UNICEF/International Child Development Centre.

Hoare, Q. and Nowell-Smith, G. (eds) (1971), *Selections from the Prison Notebooks of Antonio Gramsci.* London: Lawrence and Wishart.

Holden, C. (2007), 'Controversy for beginners: how to keep calm and maintain control while teaching about controversial issues'. Commissioned research article published online by CitizED: www.citized.info.

Huddleston, T. and Kerr, D. (eds) (2006), *Making Sense of Citizenship: A Continuing Professional Development Handbook.* London: Hodder Murray.

Jerome, L. (2003), *Assessment in Citizenship Education.* Workshop booklet. Nottingham: Anglia Polytechnic University.

Kerr, D., Lopes, J., Nelson, J., White, K., Cleaver, E. and Benton, T. (2007), *VISION versus PRAGMATISM: Citizenship in the Secondary School Curriculum in England. Citizenship Education Longitudinal Study: Fifth Annual Report.* (DfES Research Report 845). London: DfES.

Kirby, I. (2006), 'The use of drama in Citizenship education'. Commissioned research article published online by CitizED: www.citized.info.

Kirby, P., Lanyon, C., Cronin, K. and Sinclair, R. (2003), *Building a Culture of Participation: Involving Children and Young People in Policy, Service Planning, Delivery and Evaluation. Handbook.* London: DfES.

Kohlberg, L. (1968), *Essays in Moral Development – Volume 1.* San Francisco: Harper and Rowe.

Kohlberg, L. (1984), *Essays in Moral Development – Volume 2.* San Francisco: Harper and Rowe.

Laming, Lord (2003), *The Victoria Climbié Inquiry.* Norwich: HMSO.

Leonard, A. (2008), 'Global school relationships: school linking and modern challenges', in Bourn, D. (ed) (2008), *Development Education: Debates and Dialogues*. London: Institute of Education, pp. 64–98.

McIntyre, D. (1972), 'Assessment and teaching', in Rubinstein, D. and Stoneman, C. (1972), *Education for Democracy*. London: Penguin.

Macpherson, W. (1999), *The Stephen Lawrence Inquiry*. Norwich: HMSO.

Mao Zedong (1966), *Selected Quotations from Chairman Mao Zedong*. Beijing: Foreign Languages Press.

Murphy, B. K. (1999), *Transforming Ourselves, Transforming the World. An Open Conspiracy for Social Change*. London: Zed Books.

Ofsted (2003), *National Curriculum Citizenship: Planning and Implementation*. HMI 1606. London: Ofsted.

Ofsted (2005), *Citizenship in Secondary Schools: Evidence from Ofsted Inspections (2003/2004)*. HMI 2335. London: Ofsted.

Ofsted (2006), *Towards Consensus? Citizenship in Secondary Schools*. HMI 2666. London: Ofsted.

Ouseley, H. (2001), *Community Pride, Not Prejudice. Making Diversity Work in Bradford*. Bradford: Bradford Vision.

Postman, N. and Weingartner, C. (1969), *Teaching as a Subversive Activity*. London: Penguin.

Potter, J. (2002), *Active Citizenship in Schools*. London: Kogan Page.

Qualifications and Curriculum Authority (1998), *Education for Citizenship and the Teaching of Democracy in Schools*. London: QCA (Crick report).

Qualifications and Curriculum Authority (1999), *The National Curriculum Key Stages 3 and 4. Handbook for Secondary Teachers in England*. London: QCA.

Qualifications and Curriculum Authority (2006), *Assessing Citizenship: Example Assessment Activities for Key Stage 3*. London: QCA.

Qualifications and Curriculum Authority (2007), *Citizenship. Programme of Study: Key Stage 3 & 4*. London: QCA.

Rischard, J. F. (2002), *High Noon: 20 Global Problems, 20 Years to Solve Them*. New York: Basic Books.

Scarman, Lord (1981), *The Scarman Report*. London: Susana De Freitas.

Speaker's Commission on Citizenship (1990), *Encouraging Citizenship*. London: HMSO.

Tickle, L. (2008), 'A change of perspective', in 'Think global', a supplement of *The Guardian*, 29/04/08.

Training and Development Agency for Schools (2007), *Guidance to Accompany the Standards for Qualified Teacher Status (QTS)*. London: TDA.

RESOURCES

Education and government

Government

Department for Schools, Children and Families (DCSF)
Sanctuary Buildings, Great Smith Street, London SW1P 3BT
Website: www.dcsf.gov.uk
Tel: 0870 000 2288

Department for Education in Northern Ireland
Rathgael House, Balloo Road, Bangor, BT19 7PR
Website: www.deni.gov.uk
Tel: 028 9127 9279

HM Inspectorate of Education (HMEI)
Denholm House, Almondvale Business Park, Almondvale Way,
Livingston EH54 6GA
Website: www.hmie.gov.uk
Tel: 01506 600 200

Office for Standards in Education, Children's Services and Skills
(OFSTED)
Royal Exchange Buildings, St Ann's Square, Manchester M2 7LA
Website: www.ofsted.gov.uk
Tel: 08456 404045

Scottish Executive Education Department
School Education, The Scottish Government, Victoria Quay,
Edinburgh EH6 6QQ
Website: www.scotland.gov.uk/Topics/Education
Tel: 0131 556 8400

Welsh Assembly Government Education and Skills
Minister for Children, Education, Lifelong Learning & Skills, Welsh
Assembly Government, Cardiff Bay, Cardiff CF99 1NA
Website: new.wales.gov.uk/topics/educationandskills
Tel: 0845 010 3300

What is an LA?

In England and Wales, **Local Authorities (LAs)** are responsible for managing all state schools within their area. Responsibilities include funding, allocation of places and teacher employment. You can locate your local LA via DSCF: www.schoolsweb.gov.uk/locate/management/lea/fylea

General Teaching Councils

What are GTCs?

The **General Teaching Councils** are independent professional bodies with statutory power to advise the government on teaching. All qualified teachers in the United Kingdom working in state schools are required to register with a GTC.

GTC for England
Whittington House, 19–30 Alfred Place, London WC1E 7EA
Website: www.gtce.org.uk
Tel: 0870 001 0308

GTC for Northern Ireland
4th Floor Albany House, 73–75 Great Victoria Street, Belfast BT2 7AF
Website: www.gtcni.org.uk
Tel: 028 9033 3390

GTC for Scotland
Clerwood House, 96 Clermiston Road, Edinburgh EH12 6UT
Website: www.gtcs.org.uk
Tel: 0131 314 6000

GTC for Wales
4th Floor, Southgate House, Wood Street, Cardiff CF10 1EW
Website: www.gtcw.org.uk
Tel: 029 20550350

Teacher training

Administration

Graduate Teacher Training Registry (GTTR) Responsible for processing applications for PGCE and PGDE courses in England, Wales and Scotland.
Rosehill, New Barn Lane, Cheltenham, Gloucestershire GL52 3LZ
Website: www.gttr.ac.uk
Tel: 0871 468 0469

Training and Development Agency for Schools (TDA) Government agency responsible for training and development of teaching workforce.
151 Buckingham Palace Road, London SW1W 9SZ
Website: www.tda.gov.uk
Tel: 0845 6000 991

Training routes

Who needs QTS?

Anyone wishing to teach in a state school in England and Wales needs to achieve **Qualified Teacher Status (QTS)**. All the training routes shown lead to QTS or equivalent.

There is no QTS in Scotland, but new teaching graduates are required to complete an induction year and register with the GTCS.

Bachelor of Education (BEd) An honours degree course in education. Courses enable students to study for their degree and complete initial teacher training at the same time. A popular choice in teaching primary school children. ⏲ 3–4 years

Graduate Teacher Programme (GTP) Trainees are employed by a school as unqualified teachers. On-the-job training is tailored to individual needs. ⏲ 1 year

Post Graduate Certificate in Education (PGCE) Trainees spend at least a third of their time studying at a Higher Education Institution and two-thirds on three or more teaching placements in local schools. Teaching placements usually last from two to seven weeks. ⏲ 1 year

Post Graduate Diploma of Education (PGDE) Similar to a PGCE, but followed by students in Scotland. ⏱ 1 year

Registered Teacher Programme (RTP) Training route for non-graduates, providing a blend of work-based teacher training and academic study enabling trainees to complete their degree and qualify as a teacher at the same time. ⏱ 2 years

School Centred Initial Teacher Training (SCITT) Trainees spend more time training in the classroom and are taught by experienced, practising teachers. Training is delivered by groups of neighbouring schools and colleges. May also lead to PGCE. ⏱ 1 year

Teach First Programme aimed to encourage top graduates to consider teaching as a career. Trainees work in challenging secondary schools receiving teacher and leadership training as well as work experience with leading employers. ⏱ 2 years

Pay and conditions

How does a new teacher's salary grow?

Newly qualified teachers are placed on the **Main Pay Scale** (**Salary Scale for Classroom Teachers** in Scotland) at a point dependent on relevant career experience. Salary increases by one increment each year subject to satisfactory performance.

England and Wales – main pay scale (from 1 September 2008)

Spine Point	Inner London	Outer London	Other
M1	£25,000	£24,000	£20,627
M2	£26,581	£25,487	£22,259
M3	£28,261	£27,065	£24,048
M4	£30,047	£28,741	£25,898
M5	£32,358	£31,178	£27,939
M6	£34,768	£33,554	£30,148

What is the STRB?

The **School Teachers' Review Body (STRB)** reports to the Secretary of State for Education making recommendations on teachers' pay and conditions in England and Wales.

What about teachers in Northern Ireland?

Teachers' pay scales in Northern Ireland are generally the same as those in England and Wales.

Scotland – salary scale for classroom teachers (From 1 April 2008)

Scale Point	Salary
0	£20,427
1	£24,501
2	£25,956
3	£27,432
4	£29,025
5	£30,864
6	£32,583

What happens when you reach the top of the scale?

In England and Wales, teachers who reach the top of the Main Pay Scale can apply to cross the 'threshold' and move to the Upper Pay Scale. In Scotland, teachers can apply to become Chartered Teachers when they reach the top of the salary scale.

Unions

Should I join a union?

Union membership is strongly recommended. Teaching is a demanding profession with many potential legal minefields. Teaching unions provide legal and professional advice, guidance and support.

What are the benefits of TUC affiliation?

Most unions are affiliated to the Trades Union Congress (TUC) and members benefit from being part of a larger organization. Independent unions typically cater for more specialized professions and are not bound by inter-union agreements or political affiliations.

Association for Citizenship Teaching (ACT) Professional subject association for those involved in Citizenship Education.
63 Gee Street, London EC1V 3RS
Website: www.teachingcitizenship.org.uk/
Tel: 020 7566 4133

Association of Teachers & Lecturers (ATL) Represents teachers and lecturers in England, Wales and Northern Ireland. TUC affiliated.
7 Northumberland Street, London WC2N 5RD
Website: www.atl.org.uk
Tel: 020 7930 6441
Members: 120,000

Educational Institute of Scotland (EIS) Largest organization of teachers and lecturers in Scotland. TUC affiliated.
46 Moray Place, Edinburgh EH3 6BH
Website: www.eis.org.uk
Tel: 0131 225 6244
Members: 59,000

National Association of Head Teachers (NAHT) Main association representing the interests of head teachers. Independent.
1 Heath Square, Boltro Road, Haywards Heath, West Sussex RH16 1BL
Website: www.naht.org.uk
Tel: 01444 472472
Members: 30,000

National Association of School Masters/Union of Women Teachers (NASUWT) Only TUC affiliated teachers' union representing teachers and head teachers in all parts of the UK.
Hillscourt Education Centre, Rose Hill, Rednal, Birmingham B45 8RS
Website: www.nasuwt.org.uk
Tel: 0121 453 6150
Members: 250,000

National Union of Teachers (NUT) Largest teaching union
representing teachers and head teachers. TUC affiliated.
Hamilton House, Mabledon Place, London WC1H 9BD
Website: www.teachers.org.uk
Tel: 020 7388 6191
Members: 270,000

University and College Union (UCU) Largest trade union
and professional association for academics, lecturers, trainers,
researchers and academic-related staff. TUC affiliated.
27 Britannia Street, London WC1X 9JP
Website: www.ucu.org.uk
Tel: 020 7837 3636
Members: 120,000

Voice – Formerly the Professional Association of Teachers (PAT)
Independent trade union representing teachers, head teachers,
lecturers, teaching assistants, technicians, administrators and
support staff, in the public and private sectors.
2 St James' Court, Friar Gate, Derby DE1 1BT
Website: www.voicetheunion.org.uk
Tel: 01332 372 337
Members: 35,000

Curriculum

Qualifications – England, Wales and Northern Ireland

SAT	Statutory Assessment Tasks
GCSE	General Certificate of Secondary Education
BTEC	Business & Technician Education Council
NVQ	National Vocational Qualification
A Level	Advanced Level
A/S	Advanced Subsidiary Level

Qualifications – Scotland

Standard Grade
Higher
Advanced Higher
SVQ Scottish Vocational Qualification

NQF and SCQF

What is the NQF?

The **National Qualifications Framework (NQF)** and **Scottish Credit and Qualifications Framework (SCQF)** group together qualifications that place similar demands on learners.

NQF and SCQF equivalent qualifications

NQF Level	Qualifications	Vocational qualifications
1	GCSE (grades D–G)	BTEC Introductory Diploma NVQ
2	GCSEs (grades A*–C)	BTEC First Diploma NVQ
3	A-Level International Baccalaureate	BTEC Diploma BTEC National
SCQF Level	Qualification	Vocational qualification
3	Foundation Standard Grade	
4	General Standard Grade	SVQ1
5	Credit Standard Grade	SVQ2
6	Higher	SVQ3
7	Advanced Higher	

Subject associations

Association for Science Education
College Lane, Hatfield, Herts AL10 9AA
Website: www.ase.org.uk
Tel: 01707 283000

Association for Teachers of Mathematics
Unit 7, Prime Industrial Park, Shaftesbury Street, Derby DE23 8YB
Website: www.atm.org.uk
Tel: 01332 346599

Centre for Information on Language Teaching and Research
3rd Floor, 111 Westminster Bridge Road, London SE1 7HR
Website: www.cilt.org.uk
Tel: 020 7379 5101

Economics and Business Studies Association (EBEA)
The Forum, 277 London Road, Burgess Hill RH15 9QU
Website: www.ebea.org.uk
Tel: 01444 240150

Geographical Association
160 Solly Street, Sheffield S1 4BF
Website: www.geography.org.uk
Tel: 0114 296 0088

Historical Association
59a Kennington Park Road, London SE11 4JH
Website: www.history.org.uk
Tel: 020 7735 3901

National Association for Advisors and Inspectors in Design and
Technology
68 Brookfield Crescent, Hampsthwaite, Harrogate HG3 2EE
Website: www.naaidt.org.uk
Tel: –

National Association for the Teaching of English (NATE)
Website: www.nate.org.uk
Tel: 0114 255 5419

RE Today
1020 Bristol Road, Selly Oak, Birmingham B29 6LB
Website: www.retoday.org.uk
Tel: 0121 472 4242

Exam boards

Assessment & Qualifications Alliance (AQA)
Guildford Office: Stag Hill House, Guildford, Surrey GU2 7XJ
Harrogate Office: 31–33 Springfield Avenue, Harrogate, North Yorkshire HG1 2HW
Manchester Office: Devas Street, Manchester, M15 6EX
Website: www.aqa.org.uk
Tel: Guildford 01483 506 506
Harrogate 01423 840 015
Manchester 0161 953 1180

Northern Ireland Council for the Curriculum, Examination and Assessment (CCEA)
29 Clarendon Road, Clarendon Dock, Belfast BT1 3BG
Website: www.ccea.org.uk
Tel: 02890 261200

City & Guilds
1 Giltspur Street, London EC1A 9DD
Website: www.cityandguilds.com
Tel: 020 7294 2800

Edexcel
Edexcel Customer Service, One90 High Holborn, London WC1V 7BH.
Website: www.edexcel.com
Tel: 0844 576 0025

London Chamber of Commerce and Industry Examinations Board
Website: www.lccieb.com
Tel: 08707 202909

Oxford, Cambridge and RSA Examinations (OCR)
1 Hills Road, Cambridge CB1 2EU
Website: www.ocr.org.uk
Tel: 01223 553 998

Scottish Qualifications Authority (SQA)
The Optima Building, 58 Robertson Street, Glasgow G2 8DQ
Website: www.sqa.org.uk
Tel: 0845 279 1000

Welsh Joint Education Committee (WJEC)
245 Western Avenue, Cardiff CF5 2YX
Website: www.wjec.co.uk
Tel: 029 2026 5000

Media
General media

BBC News	www.bbc.co.uk/learning/subjects/schools
Daily Telegraph	www.telegraph.co.uk/education
Guardian	education.guardian.co.uk
Independent	www.independent.co.uk/news/education
Times	www.timesonline.co.uk/tol/life_and_style/education
TES	www.tes.co.uk

Teachers' TV

Freesat	650
Freeview	88
Sky	880
Tiscali TV	845
Virgin TV	240

Lesson planning
Learning styles
What is a learning style?
A learning style is the method of educating which best suits an individual. Teachers are encouraged to assess and adapt to the learning styles of their pupils. Common learning style definitions are shown below.

Auditory – learning occurs through hearing the spoken word
Kinaesthetic – learning occurs through doing and interacting
Visual – learning occurs through looking at images, demonstrations and body language

Assessment

Formative

Teachers use their assessments (observation, homework, discussion etc.) to adapt teaching and learning to meet student needs. Characterized as assessment for learning.

Summative

Students sit a test to assess their progress over a given period. Characterized as assessment of learning.

Inclusion – SEN and other barriers to learning

What do we mean by SEN pupils?

The DCSF defines students with **Special Educational Needs (SEN)** as having 'learning difficulties or disabilities which make it harder for them to learn or access education than most other children of the same age'. **School Special Educational Needs Co-ordinators (SENCO)** are responsible for coordinating SEN provision within a school.

Attention Deficit (Hyperactivity) Disorder (ADHD) Students have difficulty focusing on a specific task. Easily distracted, they have a very short attention span and have trouble commencing work. Those with hyperactivity may act impulsively and erratically.

Autistic Spectrum Disorder (ASD) Students share three main areas of difficulty: (i) social communication; (ii) social interaction; and (iii) social imagination. The condition affects students in different ways, hence use of the word 'spectrum'.

Asperger Syndrome Form of autism associated with more intellectually able individuals.

Dyscalculia Students have difficulty acquiring mathematical skills. They may have difficulty understanding simple number concepts and lack an intuitive grasp of numbers.

Dyslexia Students have a marked and persistent difficulty in learning to read, write and spell. They may have poor reading comprehension, handwriting and punctuation skills.

Dyspraxia Students are affected by an impairment or immaturity of the organization of movement and often appear clumsy. They may have poor balance and coordination. Their articulation may also be immature and their language late to develop.

English as an Additional Language (EAL)/English as a Secondary Language (ESL) Students whose main language at home (mother tongue) is a language other than English.

Emotional/Behavioural Disorder (EBD) Students' behaviour provides a barrier to their learning despite implementation of effective school behaviour policy.

Hearing Impairment (HI) Students with a hearing impairment range from those with a mild hearing loss to those who are profoundly deaf.

Individual Education Plan (IEP) Document setting out additional support and strategies provided to meet the needs of a student with learning difficulties.

Moderate Learning Difficulty (MLD) In comparison with their peers, students have much greater difficulty acquiring basic literacy and numeracy skills and in understanding concepts. Other difficulties include low self-esteem, low levels of concentration and under-developed social skills.

Multi-Sensory Impairment (MSI) Students have a combination of visual and hearing difficulties. They may also have additional disabilities.

Physical Disability (PD) Students with a visual, mobility or orthopaedic impairment that impacts on their ability to access the curriculum.

Profound and Multiple Learning Difficulty (PMLD) In addition to very severe learning difficulties, students have other significant difficulties, such as physical disabilities, sensory impairment or a severe medical condition.

Severe Learning Difficulty (SLD) Students have significant intellectual or cognitive impairments. This has a major effect on their ability to participate in the school curriculum without support.

Specific Learning Difficulty (SpLD) Umbrella term used to cover a range of difficulties including dyslexia, dyscalculia and dyspraxia.

National SEN associations

British Dyslexia Association
Unit 8, Bracknell Beeches, Old Bracknell Lane, Bracknell RG12 7BW
Website: www.bdadyslexia.org.uk
Tel: 0845 251 9002

National Attention Deficit Disorder Information and Support Service
PO Box 340, Edgware, Middlesex HA8 9HL
Website: www.addiss.co.uk
Tel: 020 8952 2800

National Association for Language Development in the Curriculum
Serif House, 10 Dudley Street, Luton LU2 0NT
Website: www.naldic.org.uk
Tel: 01582 724724

National Autistic Society
393 City Road, London EC1V 1NG
For regional contact details please visit the website.
Website: www.autism.org.uk
Tel: 020 7833 2299

National Association for Special Educational Needs
Nasen House, Amber Business Village, Amber Close, Amington, Tamworth, Staffs B77 4RP
Website: www.nasen.org.uk
Tel: 01827 311500

Dyspraxia Foundation
West Alley, Hitchin, Herts SG5 1EG
Website: www.dyspraxiafoundation.org.uk
Tel: 01462 454 986

Royal National Institute for the Deaf
19–23 Featherstone Street, London EC1Y 8SL
Website: www.rnid.org.uk
Tel: 0808 808 0123

Lesson plans

What should be included?

Many schools and universities have their own recommended lesson plan format. The suggested structure below provides a possible structure and key areas of content.

Teacher	Date	Subject	
Class	No. pupils	Ability/level	
	No. SEN pupils	LSA Support	Y/N

Context	*An introduction to . . . / Builds on material covered in a previous lesson . . .* *A cooperative/challenging class . . . strategies employed include . . .*		
Aim	*Why do we . . .* *What is the link between . . .*		
Objectives	*Understand key features of . . .* *Learn how to . . .*		
Outcomes	*Write down five facts about . . .* *Identify the key features of . . .*	**Key words**	
		Teaching activity	**Pupil activities**
Structure	Starter		*Work in pairs* *Recall previous lesson*
	Main Body		*Complete exercise* *Work in pairs*
	Plenary		*Write down* *Discuss*

Differentiation	*Extension questions* *Peer support*		
Assessment	*Teacher-led Q&A – targeted and open questions* *Marking books*		
Resources	*Textbooks, PowerPoint*		
LSA Support	*Focus on pupil x* *Circulate among all pupils*		
SEN pupils	Name	Condition	Strategy
		Dyslexia	Key words on board LSA help writing h/w

Other useful websites

A to Z of School Leadership and Management
Advice on legislation concerning schools, and guidance on a range
of school-management issues.
www.teachernet.gov.uk/atoz

Addresses of LAs in England with websites
A comprehensive list of LA contacts, news, information and
communications from the DCSF.
www.dfes.gov.uk/localauthorities

Advanced Skills Teachers
Information from TeacherNet for teachers who wish to apply.
www.teachernet.gov.uk/professionaldevelopment/opportunities/ast

BBC Key Stage 2 Revisewise bitesize revision
Revision work for Key Stage 2 students in English, Mathematics and
Science from the BBC Education website.
www.bbc.co.uk/schools/revisewise

BECTA – British Educational Communities and Technology agency
The UK government's leading agency for Information and
Communications Technology (ICT) in education.
www.becta.org.uk

Behaviour and Attendance
Information about the government's programme to improve pupil
behaviour and attendance.
www.dfes.gov.uk/behaviourandattendance/index.cfm

Birmingham Grid for Learning
The public portal contains resources and links for learners, teachers,
parents and administrators.
www.bgfl.org/bgfl

Building Bridges
Information on the Independent/State School Partnerships Grant
Scheme, set up to encourage collaborative working between
independent and maintained schools.
www.dfes.gov.uk/buildingbridges

CEGNET
Careers education website from the Connexions Service National
Unit for schools and colleges and their partners.
www.cegnet.co.uk

Children and Young People's Unit
The website of the government unit for the better coordination of
policies and services for children.
www.allchildrenni.gov.uk

Choice
First online course prospectus for 14 to 19 year olds in London.
Includes a free searchable directory of over 25,000 courses, with
clear details of all the learning opportunities open to young people.
www.yourlondon.gov.uk/choice

Citizenship
The DCSF citizenship website, which includes schemes of work and
teaching resources, plus articles and information from assessment to
whole-school issues.
www.dfes.gov.uk/citizenship

Code of Practice on LA-School Relations
Link to a downloadable version of the code, providing statutory
guidance on how to raise standards.
www.dfes.gov.uk/lea

Connecting Voices (COVO)
A Southwark-based charity delivering services that address conflict, disaffection and under-achievement in education and the workplace.
www.covo.org.uk

Connexions
Guidance and support for 13 to 19 year olds in all areas of life.
www.connexions.gov.uk

Curriculum Online
A comprehensive catalogue of digital learning resources for the National Curriculum for England.
www.curriculumonline.gov.uk

Don't Suffer in Silence
Website showing pupils, their families and teachers how to tackle bullying problems.
www.dfes.gov.uk/bullying

Education Protects
A project funded by the DCSF aiming to help raise the educational achievements of children and young people in care.
www.dfes.gov.uk/educationprotects

DCSF – Languages Strategy
The Languages for Life website outlining the government's Languages plans to transform language use and acquisition.
www.dfes.gov.uk/languagesstrategy

Directgov
Main portal for access to UK government services, including the latest, up-to-date public-service information.
www.direct.gov.uk

Every Child Matters: Change for Children
Useful materials and case studies to help understand and deliver the Every Child Matters agenda.
www.everychildmatters.gov.uk

Fast Track
Accelerated leadership development programme for new teachers.
www.dfee.gov.uk/fasttrack

Global Gateway
Information for the development of an international dimension
in education. Including ideas for lesson plans, free downloadable
resources, an area for young people and information on gap years.
www.globalgateway.org

Go-Givers
Site showing primary children what it means to be part of a caring
society. Including case studies for assemblies, discussion activities
and a range of resources ideal for teaching Citizenship.
www.gogivers.org

Homework – The Standards Site
Support for the development of independent learning skills and
attitudes for successful lifelong learning.
www.standards.dfes.gov.uk/homework

Key Stage 3: The Standards Site
Information on the Key Stage 3 curriculum standards.
www.standards.dfee.gov.uk/keystage3

Learning and Skills Council
Information and guidance on further education, work-based
training, entry to employment and modern apprenticeships.
www.lsc.gov.uk

Learning and Skills Development Agency
National resource for the development of policy and practice in
post-16 education and training.
www.lsda.org.uk

LifeBytes
Website for 11 to 14 year olds providing facts and information about
their health.
www.lifebytes.gov.uk

Literacy: The Standards Site
Support for teachers and educational professionals to improve
literacy in schools.
www.standards.dfes.gov.uk/primary/literacy

National Vocational Qualifications
Information on NVQs and the career opportunities they provide.
www.dfes.gov.uk/nvq

Numeracy: The Standards Site
Support for teachers and educational professionals to improve
numeracy in schools.
www.standards.dfes.gov.uk/primary/mathematics

Practical Research for Education
Online journal for education students, teachers and education
lecturers. Includes free articles, profile interviews with researchers
and a forum to discuss educational research.
www.pre-online.co.uk

Primary National Strategy
Support from the DCSF for all aspects of primary teaching.
www.standards.dfes.gov.uk/primary

Qualifications and Curriculum Authority (QCA)
Website of the QCA, the governing body who maintain and develop
the school curriculum and assessments and accredit and monitor
qualifications.
www.qca.org.uk

School Lookup
Access to the DCSF EduBase database of all nurseries, schools and
colleges in the UK.
www.easea.co.uk

SEN
Special Educational Needs page from TeacherNet offering
information on SEN including materials for teachers, parents and
other education professionals.
www.dfes.gov.uk/sen

Standards Site
Internet materials and services aiming to support and improve
teacher ability and raise levels of achievement.
www.standards.dfes.gov.uk

TeacherNet
Education website for teachers and school managers, setting the government standard for UK teachers and schools-related professions. Including resources, lesson plans and assessment strategies.
www.teachernet.gov.uk

Teachers' Pension Scheme
Information about the Teachers' Pensions Scheme for England and Wales.
www.teacherspensions.co.uk

Teacher Xpress
Resources and links to educational websites covering every area of the curriculum.
www.teacherxpress.com

Times Educational Supplement
Jobs, resources and ideas for all teachers and people working in education. Resource Bank section includes a large section of resources for teachers by teachers.
www.tes.co.uk

References

ATL	www.atl.org.uk
BBC.co.uk	www.bbc.co.uk/health
British Dyslexia Association	www.bdadyslexia.org.uk
DCSF	www.dcsf.gov.uk
Directgov	www.direct.gov.uk
Educational Resources.co.uk	www.educationalresources.co.uk
GTC England	www.gtce.org.uk
GTC Northern Ireland	www.gtcni.org.uk
GTTR	www.gttr.ac.uk
Info Scotland: Teaching in Scotland	www.teachinginscotland.com
NASUWT	www.nasuwt.org.uk

National Autistic Society	www.autism.org.uk
NUT	www.teachers.org.uk
Scottish Credit and Qualifications Network	www.scqf.org.uk
Scottish Executive Education Department	www.scotland.gov.uk/Topics/Education
TeacherNet	www.teachernet.gov.uk
EIS	www.eis.org.uk
TDA	www.tda.gov.uk
TUC	www.tuc.org.uk
UCU	www.ucu.org.uk
Voice	www.voicetheunion.org.uk

Index

Page references in *italic* refer to information found in figures
Page references in **bold** refer to information found in practitioner reflections